TREKKING THE GR10

TREKKING THE GR10

THROUGH THE FRENCH PYRENEES:
LE SENTIER DES PYRENEES

by Brian Johnson and Stuart Butler

JUNIPER HOUSE, MURLEY MOSS,
OXENHOLME ROAD, KENDAL, CUMBRIA LA9 7RL
www.cicerone.co.uk

© Brian Johnson and Stuart Butler 2023
Second Editon 2023
ISBN: 978 1 78631 116 0
First edition 2016

Replaces guide of same title by Paul Lucia (ISBN: 978 1 85284 364 9)

Printed in Turkey by Pelikan Basim using responsibly sourced paper.
A catalogue record for this book is available from the British Library.
All photographs are by the authors.

Route mapping by Lovell Johns www.lovelljohns.com
Contains OpenStreetMap.org data © OpenStreetMap
contributors, CC-BY-SA. NASA relief data courtesy of ESRI

The routes of the GR®, PR® and GRP® paths in this guide
have been reproduced with the permission of the Fédération
Française de la Randonnée Pédestre holder of the exclusive
rights of the routes. The names GR®, PR® and GRP® are registered trademarks.
© FFRP 2016 for all GR®, PR® and GRP® paths appearing in this work.

Updates to this Guide

While every effort is made by our authors to ensure the accuracy of guidebooks
as they go to print, changes can occur during the lifetime of an edition. Any
updates that we know of for this guide will be on the Cicerone website (www.
cicerone.co.uk/1116/updates), so please check before planning your trip.
We also advise that you check information about such things as transport,
accommodation and shops locally. Even rights of way can be altered over time.
We are always grateful for information about any discrepancies between a
guidebook and the facts on the ground, sent by email to updates@cicerone.co.uk
or by post to Cicerone, Juniper House, Murley Moss, Oxenholme Road, Kendal,
LA9 7RL.

Register your book: To sign up to receive free updates, special offers and
GPX files where available, create a Cicerone account and register your purchase
via the 'My Account' tab at www.cicerone.co.uk.

Front cover: The iconic Pic du Midi d'Ossau as seen from the Lac Gentau (Stage 13)

CONTENTS

Spectacular landscapes abound around the small village of Lescun, which is passed on Stages 11 and 12

Symbols used on route maps

⟨↑⟩	start point
⟨↑⟩	finish point
⟨S⟩	alternative start point
⟨F⟩	alternative finish point
∿	route
⚊ ⚊ ⚊	alternative route
••••••	optional route
═══	road
═══	motorway
━■━	station/railway
⌁	minor track or path
⌁	minor track or dirt road
∿	river
∿	regional border
∿	international border
	glacier
	woodland
	urban areas
● ○	settlement
▲	summit
⤬	saddle/col
■	significant building
⌂	accommodation
⌂	bothy (unmanned refuge)
⊗	campground
⚑	aire de bivouac
⊗	bar/restaurant
ⓘ	tourist info office
⊛	food shop
Ⓦ	water
╱	chairlift

Relief
in metres

3400–3600	
3200–3400	
3000–3200	
2800–3000	
2600–2800	
2400–2600	
2200–2400	
2000–2200	
1800–2000	
1600–1800	
1400–1600	
1200–1400	
1000–1200	
800–1000	
600–800	
400–600	
200–400	
0–200	

SCALE: 1:100,000

0 kilometres 1   2

0 miles   1

Contour lines are drawn
at 50m intervals and
highlighted at 200m
intervals.

Lacs d'Embarrat, a string of beautiful lakes that can be passed on Stage 17A

Mountain safety

Every mountain walk has its dangers, and those described in this guidebook are no exception. All who walk or climb in the mountains should recognise this and take responsibility for themselves and their companions along the way. The author and publisher have made every effort to ensure that the information contained in this guide was correct when it went to press, but, except for any liability that cannot be excluded by law, they cannot accept responsibility for any loss, injury or inconvenience sustained by any person using this book.

International distress signal *(emergency only)*
Six blasts on a whistle (and flashes with a torch after dark) spaced evenly for one minute, followed by a minute's pause. Repeat until an answer is received. The response is three signals per minute followed by a minute's pause.

Helicopter rescue
The following signals are used to communicate with a helicopter:

Help needed: raise both arms above head to form a 'Y'

Help not needed: raise one arm above head, extend other arm downward

Emergency telephone numbers
Emergency services: tel 112

Weather reports
Meteo France: www.meteo.fr

Mountain rescue can be very expensive – be adequately insured.

A rare late winter snowfall on the Crete d'Iparla (Stage 4)

AUTHOR'S PREFACE

Having lived in the shadow of the western Pyrenees for more than a quarter of a century (gulp!) and walked literally thousands of kilometres of different mountain trails here, the Pyrenees are a mountain range very close to my heart. In fact, in my somewhat biased opinion, they are the most beautiful mountain range in the world and a place I will never tire of. So, it was a huge pleasure to be asked by Cicerone to update this guide to the epic GR10 trans-Pyrenees trail. However, it was a pleasure tinged with sadness as I would be taking the reins of previous author, Brian Johnson. A legend in walker's circles, Brian was the author of numerous hiking guidebooks and I myself had used several of his guides (including this very book) on my own hiking adventures. Sadly, though, Brian died in 2021. It was an honour – and a huge responsibility – to be asked to continue Brian's legacy by updating this book. I hope he would have been pleased with the results.

The first Cicerone guide to the GR10 was actually written by Alan Castle and published in 1990. His work was taken on by Paul Lucia, whose new guide was published in 2002. Unfortunately, Paul also died in 2007. His work was then updated by Ton Joosten, before Brian took over.

Over the years things have changed on the GR10. It has become far better known and more popular since the first edition of this book was produced. Indeed, since the Covid pandemic there has been an explosion of people taking to mountain trails the world over, the GR10 included. Although it's just about possible to walk the GR10 without camping or using bothies – and this guide is organised into 55 stages for the benefit of those who are using accommodation along the route – it does involve some careful pre-planning and advance accommodation reservations. Since 2020 mountain refuges in particular have generally been booked solid all summer. Walkers who prefer wild camping in the mountains will find much greater flexibility in their planning.

Stuart Butler

Mont Valier from ponds below the Bouche d'Aula (Stage 34)

INTRODUCTION

The north face of Vignemale from Oulètes de Gaube (Stages 18 and 19)

The Pyrenees, the mountain chain which forms the border between France and Spain, stretch over 400km from the Atlantic Ocean to the Mediterranean Sea, and at Pico Aneto (entirely within Spain) they reach their highest point at an ice-frosted 3404m. These statisitics clearly show that the Pyrenees aren't one of Europe's bigger mountain ranges, but what they don't show is that what the Pyrenees might lack in altitude they more than make up for in beauty. For the Pyrenees are, unquestionably, one of Europes prettiest and most diverse mountain ranges. Thousands of lakes of all shapes and sizes sprawl amongst Alpine flower meadows full of butterflies and sheep.

Imposing slabs of rock reach toward glaciated summits and lower down, ancient, dense beech forests turn a firey orange in autumn and quaint farming villages, where ancient traditions hold strong, populate lush, green valley floors.

The GR10 is a superb long distance trail that runs across the entiety of the French side of these mountains from the Atlantic to Mediterranean.

It is an extremely well-waymarked route following good mountain paths, with only a few tough stages with boulderfields to cross and occasional scrambling. Towns and villages are frequent so finding accommodation and supplies is rarely a problem.

Initially the GR10 follows ridges over the steep rolling hills of the Basque Country before reaching the impressive limestone peaks at the western end of the High Pyrenees. The scenery reaches a crescendo in the High Pyrenees where rugged terrain, plunging valleys, lofty lookouts and massive mountain cirques mark the route. After the town of Bagnères-de-Luchon the GR10 passes into the less-frequented Ariège where the route crosses a succession of deep valleys with occasional returns to spectacular Alpine terrain. As the Mediterranean is approached the Canigou massif dominates the scene and the terrain remains mountainous with the final 1000m peak being only a few miles from the route's end at Banyuls-sur-Mer.

The highlight of the GR10 for many walkers isn't the mountains or the fauna (as diverse as this is), but the magnificent wildflower meadows and shimmering lakes in which great peaks are reflected. This is an unforgettable walk through a stunning mountain range.

THE STAGES

At 954km in length with a total climb of 53,000m, taking approximately 315 hours to complete, the GR10 is too long for most hikers to do in a single trip and most will break it up into sections and walk it over several years. There are good bus and rail links throughout the French Pyrenees

so there is plenty of choice when splitting into sections. For convenience, this guide has been divided into four sections, which fit in well with the rail links. See Appendix A for a route summary table.

For a fit walker, it would be possible to complete the entire trek in around 45 days by combining stages. This would require some planning ahead to ensure daily distances are realistic and accommodation options fit the intended schedule. It would also require the weather to be reliably on your side and wouldn't allow for many diversions off the main route, which would be a great pity as these diversions and side trails often lead to the most rewarding experiences and memories. Therefore, we would suggest adding in an extra week at the least.

Section 1: Hendaye-Plage to Etsaut (Stages 1–12)

As the GR10 leaves the border town of Hendaye on the Atlantic coast it follows ridges over the steep, grassy and wooded rolling hills of the Basque Country. After nine stages there is a rapid transition to the steep limestone peaks at the western end of the High Pyrenees. Section totals: 221km; 11,300m; 68 hours.

Section 2: Etsaut to Bagnères-de-Luchon (Stages 13–26)

This is the most spectacular section of the GR10, passing through the High Pyrenees, which rise to

Pont d'Espagne (Stage 18)

over 3000m, crossing high passes that may be snow-covered well into summer. The fantastic scenery in this section reaches its visual highlights as you pass around the Pic du Midi d'Ossau, Vignemale, Gavarnie and the Néouvielle massif. Section totals: 253km; 14,400m ascent; 85 hours.

Section 3: Bagnères-de-Luchon to Mérens-les-Vals (Stages 27–43)

In this section, the border between France and Spain (or Andorra) is well north of the watershed and the GR10 passes through the Ariège. These mountains aren't quite as high as the High Pyrenees, but the route crosses a succession of deep valleys cut out by the huge glaciers that flowed north from the Pyrenees in the last Ice Age, meaning that there is a lot of ascent. The Ariège has never been as popular as the High Pyrenees so there is often a feeling of remoteness as you walk through a land of deep forests and across pastures where a traditional shepherding life-style remains strong. This region is also a stronghold for brown bears and other wildlife. Facilities for walkers are harder to find. Section totals: 265km; 17,600m ascent; 98 hours.

Section 4: Mérens-les-Vals to Banyuls-sur-Mer (Stages 44–55)

The first few days of this section are through spectacular Alpine terrain, after which the mountains become gentler. After the dominating Canigou massif is passed, the terrain becomes drier and notably more Mediterranean but remains mountainous, with the final 1000m peak being only a few miles from Banyuls-sur-Mer. Section totals: 215km; 9700m ascent; 64 hours.

THE ROUTE

The GR10 doesn't pass over many summits but suggestions are made in the route descriptions for climbing many of the easier peaks along the route, often from cols over which the route passes. If you want to climb some of the higher, more difficult peaks you should ask for advice from the guardians of the refuges.

It would be possible to walk the GR10 from the Mediterranean to Atlantic, but this guide describes the route from the Atlantic so that you have the prevailing wind/rain on your back and you have time to acclimatise to the heat before reaching the Mediterranean, with the added advantage that in hot weather the steep climbs can often be done in the shade of early morning.

The author noted a lot of minor changes to the route in 2022 as the Fédération Française de la Randonnée Pédestre (FFRP) are continually trying to make improvements, so don't be surprised if the trail on the ground doesn't always match the route description. However, route changes are well waymarked and can be followed with confidence.

FROM THE ATLANTIC TO THE MEDITERRANEAN

The Pyrenees are traversed by three long-distance routes coast to coast: the GR10, the High-level Route (Haute Randonnée Pyrénéenne, HRP) and the GR11 (la Senda Pirenaica). All three routes provide varied and scenic treks through magnificent, often remote, high or deserted mountains. The GR11 stays higher and is rougher than the GR10, but there is actually more ascent on the GR10. Unless you are an experienced mountaineer you should opt for the GR10 or GR11 over the HRP.

This guide covers the GR10, which remains in France and stays north of the watershed. Well way-marked and following good mountain paths, it is the easiest of the three routes. Although much time is spent climbing up and down steep forested ridges, time is spent above the treeline on every stage. You are able to camp throughout, but it is not a necessity due to the frequent visits to towns and villages and a network of hostel-style accommodation in gîtes d'étape or refuges.

The HRP, which passes through France, Spain and Andorra, is not so much a walk as a mountaineering expedition. The route is not way-marked, except where it coincides with other routes, and you must expect to get lost! There is a lot of very rough terrain, including some very steep, possibly dangerous descents. Visits to towns and villages are infrequent so resupply is difficult and you will have to camp much of the time. You will spend a lot of time on high mountain ridges with serious risk of thunderstorms and even fresh snow. The HRP is particularly demanding in bad weather or in early summer when snow could mean serious winter mountaineering skills are required. The HRP is a daunting route for the inexperienced but is a magnificent expedition for those with the right experience.

A Patou sheep dog guarding a flock of sheep

Clockwise from top left: great white Arum lily; Great yellow gentian; Sedum arachnoideum; Pasque; Musk mallow

The GR11 is a well waymarked mountain path, which passes through Spain and Andorra. Like the HRP, it crosses many high mountain passes where there are boulderfields, scree and some easy scrambling at about the maximum difficulty the inexperienced would want when carrying a heavy rucksack. Thunderstorms are less of a problem than on the HRP as you don't spend long periods on high ridges. Frequent visits to towns and villages mean that resupply isn't much of a problem. Those who prefer not to camp or bivouac will find that a few of the stages are rather long and that some alternative routes will need to be taken.

WILDLIFE

The Pyrenees are one of the few places where populations of almost all large animals are now actually increasing and spotting the wildlife of the range will quickly become a real highlight for most people. The birdwatching here is fantastic with the mountain range forming a big barrier to migrating birds, in the spring and autumn they are funnelled along the Atlantic and Mediterranean coastlines and through the lower passes. The casual birdwatcher will be most impressed with the large number of birds of prey (the western end of the range is the best area for raptors).

The massive griffon vulture, with a wing-span of about 2.5m, will frequently be seen, and often in large numbers, soaring above the high ridges. The bearded vulture, a massive bird with a habit for dropping bones from a great height in order to smash them and get at the marrow within, was once very rare here, but is now easy to see in many parts of the central Pyrenees. While the smaller, and much less common, Egyptian vulture, which is distinctively coloured with a white body and black-and-white wings, might also be seen. The majestic golden eagle is also fairly common but can be hard for the novice to identify as it cruises past at high altitude. The red kite is a beautiful bird with a deeply forked tail. You can also expect to see black kites, buzzards and honey buzzards, as well as smaller birds of prey such as the kestrel, peregrine falcon, sparrowhawk and rarer birds such as the black-shouldered kite (a recent arrival from North Africa but one that is becoming increasingly established), the goshawk and even a migrating osprey.

One species, which seems to be thriving, is the Alpine chough, seen in large flocks. This member of the crow family is all black except for a yellow bill and red legs. Wheatear and black redstart are common, and rarer small birds to look out for are the wallcreeper, crossbill, crested tit, red-backed shrike, bullfinch and Alpine accentor. Another recent, and wholly unexpected, arrival is the Red-billed leiothrix, a tiny but impossible to miss and highly colourful bird that originates from Tibet and the Himalaya!

There are a number of colonies established in Pyrenean valleys.

You will have sightings of chamois (isard/izard), which was hunted to near extinction but is now recovering well and are commonly seen in quite large herds. Other mammals you will see include lots of marmots (that whistling noise you might hear as you cross a meadow is the alarm call of marmots, which you'll see darting into their burrows seconds later), several species of deer, fox, red squirrel and the reintroduced mouflon and ibex. There are loads of badgers and wild boar but being nocturnal these are less likely to be seen.

Brown bears have been reintroduced to the Ariège and Béarn and the latest census indicates there are around 70 individuals, but it is extremely unlikely that you will see one and if you do it will almost certainly be running away from you!

You are likely to see many reptiles and amphibians including several species of snake, lizard, toad, frog and the dramatic fire salamander, which in the Pyrenees has yellow stripes rather than spots.

THE WEATHER AND WHEN TO GO

The hills of the Basque Country and Navarre have a reputation for mist and spells of gentle rain, but temperatures above 40°C are not unknown. (Anyone who walked the GR10 during the summer of 2022 will be able

Pic de la Mede seen from the descent from Col d'Auéran (Stage 29)

to testify to this!) In the High Pyrenees and the Ariège you are to the north of the watershed and with the prevailing wind coming from the northwest, it is not uncommon to get damp, cloudy weather. If you are lucky there will be long spells of warm sunny weather.

These are high mountains and can be subject to terrific thunderstorms. Thunderstorms in high mountains are usually thought of as being an afternoon phenomenon, but in the Pyrenees the storms are often slow to build up and can arrive in the evening or even in the middle of the night. In the past these summer thunderstorms followed a fairly reliable pattern. The temperature and humidity would build up over the course of three or four days before the heavens opened in dramatic and, if you were unlucky enough to be caught out on an exposed pass at the time, scary fashion. The following morning would then dawn cloudy and cooler before the sun burst through and the pattern repeated. Over the last few years through this pattern has become far less predictable and thunderstorms less common, but when they occur it can be at any moment of the day and year. As the Mediterranean is approached the weather will tend to be sunnier and drier, but you must still be prepared for rain. Summer snowfall is very unusual, but in the past snow has fallen as low as 1500m on the GR10 in August.

Snow conditions vary tremendously from year to year, but the general pattern is heading toward a shorter and less snowy winter. Ski resorts are starting to face real problems. Unless you have confirmed it is a low snow year, the inexperienced would be advised to wait for early to mid-June or July before setting off from Hendaye. The berger (shepherd) at the Cabane de la Subera advises that you should not attempt the GR10 in the Ariège until mid July in an average snow year.

The best months to walk the GR10 are mid and late June, July, August and September, but if you are only intending to walk sections of the GR10 in the Basque Country, you may prefer May, June or October when the weather will be cooler. July and August are hot and busy throughout the range and the later into summer you go the more parched the countryside becomes. If you really want to see the Pyrenees at their absolute best then October, when the skies are clear, the weather often perfect, a light dusting of fresh snow lies on high summits and the autumnal colours in the beech forests are divine, can be unbeatable. However, trying to complete the entire GR10 in October would be very ambitious and should not be attempted by anyone without experience in snow and winter weather. Also, most of the refuges are unstaffed by October so you'd need to be self-sufficient. You should be aware that the main holiday season is July and August and that some facilities are only open during those two months.

See Appendix C for a list of weather-related websites to visit for forecasts, weather warnings and advice.

GETTING THERE AND BACK

Access to the GR10 will be by car, bus, train or plane. Useful websites are given in Appendix C.

Car

You could drive down through France or take the car ferry from Portsmouth or Plymouth to Santander in northern Spain and then leave it parked up somewhere. It will be much safer to leave your car in the mountains and then take the train to Hendaye to start your walk rather than leave your car unattended for long periods in popular seaside resorts. However, wherever you leave it, a foreign-registered car parked in the same place for a long period of time might raise suspicions so this option is probably best avoided.

Bus

It is possible to reach the Pyrenees by overnight bus from London (Victoria Coach Station). National Express run links to London and then FlixBus run buses throughout Europe. The most convenient destination for those walking the GR10 is Irún (in Spain). FlixBus also operate services to Bayonne, Orthez, Pau, Tarbes, Saint-Gaudens, Toulouse and Perpignan. The journey time is long and the cost not that much less than taking the train or flying.

GR10 hikers on the approach to Col d'Auéran (Stage 29)

Rail and bus

Paris can be reached by Eurostar. From there OuiSNCF run high-speed trains to a variety of destinations including Hendaye, Toulouse and Perpignan. The main west–east line joins Hendaye, Bayonne, Pau, Lourdes, Tarbes, Toulouse and Perpignan.

From **Bayonne** there are local trains to Bidarray and Saint-Jean-Pied-de-Port, from where there are buses to Sare and St-Étienne-de-Baïgorry.

From **Pau** you can take a train to Oloron-Ste-Marie then bus to Etsaut or Arette-la Pierre-St-Martin. From Pau there are buses to Larun and connections to Gabas and Gourette.

From **Lourdes** there are buses to Argelès-Gazost with connections to Arrens-Marsous, Cauterets, Luz-Saint-Sauveur, Barèges and Gavarnie.

From **Tarbes** there are trains to St-Lary-Soulan connecting with buses to Vielle-Aure, or trains to Bagnères-de-Luchon (via Montréjeau).

From **St-Girons** there are bus services to Sentein, Les Bordes-sur-Lez, Seix, St-Lizier and Aulas-les-bains with connections to Toulouse.

From **Toulouse** there are trains to Latour-de-Carol passing through Tarascon-sur-Ariège, from where there are buses to Auzat and Mérens-les-Vals.

There is also a rail link from Perpignan to Villefranche, and onward by narrow gauge railway, Train Jaune, via la Cabanasse, to Latour-de-Carol. Alternatively there is a direct bus link from Perpignan to Latour-de-Carol crossing the GR10 at the Col de la Perche. There is a bus service from Perpignan to Arles-sur-Tech and le Perthus.

At the end of your walk there is a good rail service between Banyuls-sur-Mer and Perpignan. Book train tickets as far in advance as possible to ensure a better price.

Plane

At the time of writing, both Ryanair and Easyjet fly from Stansted and some regional airports to Biarritz, Carcassonne and Perpignan, and British Airways fly direct to Toulouse. Air France has flights from London to Pau and a big choice of destinations if you fly via Paris. You could also take a flight to Bilbao in Spain from where it's just an hour by regular bus to San Sebastián followed by a 25min local train ride (Euskotren; http://euskotren. eus) to Hendaye.

EQUIPMENT

The GR10 is a serious expedition so you should have previous experience of backpacking or long-distance walking before attempting this fantastic route. A few general points are made on equipment here.

- Keep your load as light as possible. If you don't need it, don't carry it!
- You will need a sheet sleeping bag or lightweight sleeping bag for use in refuges or some gîtes d'étape.

If you are using accommodation you may still want to carry a sleeping bag and camping mat to enable you to bivouac when required.

- Your waterproofs should be able to cope with thunderstorms and heavy rain.
- Shorts are the preferred legwear of most hikers in the high summer.
- A sun hat is strongly recommended and you should use plenty of sun-screen.
- Good quality lightweight boots or sturdy walking shoes are the best footwear. Heavy boots aren't necessary and trainers won't be robust enough for the terrain. Make sure they have a good tread.
- Be warned that even in summer it can get cold at night. On some of the higher elevation night stops the temperature can drop to almost zero, even in August, so you'll want a fleece, and a thermal is a good, light-weight, addition.
- If you are camping you should have, as a minimum, containers capable of carrying three litres of water.
- It is strongly recommended that you use two walking poles. Mini-spikes or even full crampons may be needed in early season in a high snow year.
- If you are carrying any electronic devices needing recharging, remember to carry a continental adaptor.

Safety
On the GR10, especially in the Ariège, you are often traversing very steep slopes where a fall could have

Tour de France riders below Barèges after descending the Col du Tourmalet (Stage 21)

fatal consequences. It is not the difficult terrain – there is very little difficult terrain on the GR10 – it is the careless slip on an easy but exposed path that is potentially dangerous. It is strongly recommended that you use two walking poles and learn to use them effectively to prevent a careless slip on a steep traverse. This is in addition to the other uses of walking poles such as crossing snowfields, stream crossings, descending steep slopes, clearing vegetation and warding off dogs. Poles might also help in the extremely unlikely event of meeting a bear or the more likely encounter with a bull, or even for use as an emergency tent pole.

CULTURE AND LANGUAGES

Spanish siesta

You may not be in Spain, but in the smaller villages you can expect shops to be open in the morning, closed during the afternoon (normally from 12.00–12.30pm to 2–2.30pm) and open again until 7–7.30pm. On Sundays almost everything will be closed. In tourist towns in high summer, though, many shops will remain open non-stop.

Languages

French is spoken throughout the French Pyrenees. In addition, the locals may also speak Basque or Catalan. English is now spoken much more widely than it was in the 20th century, especially by younger people.

There is a lot of confusion with place names in the Pyrenees, with many different and inconsistent spellings. Villages, towns and geographical features often have a French name, a Basque or Catalan name and possibly a Spanish name.

In this guide, the French name has been used unless the Basque or Catalan name is in widespread use.

Politics

When they were independent states the Basque Country and Catalonia were much larger than at present and included large chunks of the Pyrenees which are now in France. Independence movements aren't as active as in Spain, but many people will still think of themselves as Basque or Catalan rather than French. Fortunately, the nationalist violence of the recent past has now ended.

Chemin de la Liberté

As you walk the GR10 you will see frequent references to Le Chemin de la Liberté. After the fall of France in 1940 there was a steady stream of military personnel, including escaped prisoners of war and Frenchmen wanting to join the allied armies, as well as persecuted civilians, including many Jews, trying to escape across the border from France into Spain. From November 1942 the security of the border was taken over by the Germans with frontier guards posted along the whole

Le Chemin de la Liberté plaque

length of the Pyrenees and a forbidden zone 20km deep was set up, into which access was only allowed with a special pass.

It then became vital to develop more efficient and certainly more secret ways of reaching safety in Spain. The result was the founding of many well-organised escape lines whose aim was to pass not only men but also important military information and documents. This was very dangerous work and more than half of the 2000 known guides were caught and either executed immediately or imprisoned to die later in concentration camps. It is estimated that 33,000 men, women and children escaped successfully to freedom.

The best known of these escape routes is Le Chemin de la Liberté, which passes through the Ariège from Saint-Girons to Alos d'Isil in Spain. When you hike the GR10 in good summer weather, remember that many of these crossings would have been made at night in appalling weather and in winter over snow-covered mountains.

Tour de France
The Tour de France cycle race visits the Pyrenees in July and may impinge on the GR10 with road closures and fully booked facilities.

ACCOMMODATION

There is a wide range of accommodation on the GR10.

- Hotels vary greatly in quality and cost but even the cheapest offer a high standard of comfort. An auberge is the equivalent of an English inn.
- Chambres d'hôtes are private houses offering accommodation similar to the British 'bed & breakfast'. They are a fantastic way to get a more intimate look at rural French life with dinner (and sometimes breakfast) often being communal affairs hosted by the owners.
- Gîtes d'étape are a network of cheap accommodation aimed primarily at walkers. They often have dormitory accommodation, but many also have smaller rooms. Most, but not all, will offer evening meals, breakfast and picnic lunches. Some will be open for snacks and drinks during the

Cabane de Besset (bothy) (Stage 31)

day. Most will have a kitchen for the use of visitors. Don't get confused by the 'gîte' designation; these are mainly chambres d'hôtes rather than gîtes d'étape.

- Manned refuges are mountain huts (today some are more like full blown hotels!) that offer accommodation, possibly in dormitories. In summer many of them have a drink and meals service, open to both residents and non-residents, and will usually provide packed lunches.
- Unmanned refuges are open year round for the use of mountaineers and walkers. They are equivalent to the Scottish 'bothy' and range in quality from purpose-built buildings, which are well maintained by mountaineering clubs, to buildings that are little better than unmaintained cow sheds. Sometimes they are in fact just cow sheds!
- Some campgrounds will have cabins, static caravans or gîte d'étape accommodation.

If desperate ask at a village bar-restaurant; they will often know locals who are willing to offer accommodation outside the official system.

It is strongly recommended that you book accommodation in advance. At some gîtes d'étape it may be necessary to book meals and picnic supplies in advance as the owners will often shop daily for fresh food. With the increasing popularity of the Pyrenees, many of the manned mountain refuges are booked solid all summer.

Manned refuges

Manned refuges vary greatly but as a guideline you can expect the following:

- Basic accommodation for walkers and climbers.
- Refuge hours and rules designed for walkers, not for late-night drinkers.
- You may be able to get a discount if you are a member of an Alpine Association.
- People staying in refuges usually book demi-pension (dinner, bed and breakfast).
- Most refuges will supply picnic lunches.
- Some, but not all, will have self-catering facilities.
- Mattresses and blankets are provided in the dormitories but you may need to bring a sheet sleeping bag. Proper sleeping bags are often forbidden.
- Almost all (there are now some exceptions) staffed refuges are only manned between about June and September, but all have a small winter quarters which is open year round and for which you will need to be self-sufficient. Some may open out of season if you're a group and make a reservation.

- It is highly recommended that you make reservations in high summer and at weekends. The increasing popularity of the Pyrenees means many manned refuges can be fully booked for the entire summer.
- Refuges offer a bar and snack service to walkers outside of normal mealtimes.
- Camping is generally permitted in designated areas next to most manned refuges. Campers can book meals at the refuge. Occasionally, there are local restrictions banning camping near a refuge.

Bothies

Cabanes were built as summer homes for the bergers (shepherds and herdsmen) who look after the sheep, cows and goats. The majority are still used for this purpose, especially during July and August. However, they may be available for use as a bothy when the shepherd is not in residence, or they may be locked. Some have a small side room available for the use of walkers.

A few of these cabanes have been adapted as permanent bothies, especially in the Ariège and Catalonia. Note that the sleeping platform is often in the roof space.

CAMPING

In this guide the American term 'campground' has been used for

'La Cascade', Gorges de Kakouéta (Stage 9)

commercial or organised campsites, to distinguish them from wilderness campsites.

In the Parc National des Pyrénées 'camping' is not allowed but you can 'bivouac' with or without a small tent between the hours of 7.00pm and 9.00am, provided you are at least one hour's walk from the access road. There are also aires de bivouac, which you may use, usually close to road access or to refuges. These are official wilderness campsites, very occasionally with toilets and water. In practice similar rules apply to other mountain areas.

Hot springs above Mérens-les-Vals (Stage 44)

There is rarely any problem camping high in the mountains but discretion should be used when camping at lower levels. You should ask permission if you want to camp near villages, in farmer's fields or close to a refuge. The daily stages given in this guide are intended for those using overnight accommodation. Those who are wild camping should ignore these stages and camp well away from the towns, villages and refuges.

If you are accustomed to always camping beside water you will sometimes have difficulty in finding suitable campsites, especially in drier eastern Catalonia. If you are prepared to camp away from water, you have much more flexibility and you can often find campsites with spectacular views.

Suggestions have been made in this guide as to the best campsites. These will normally be places where camping is legal, where there is good drainage and good grass which will take a tent peg. The best campsites are often on passes, but these will be very exposed in windy weather or thunderstorms. The experienced backpacker will find plenty of other places to camp.

It is often preferable to camp high in the mountains as it's legal and there is less chance of being disturbed. There will be fewer cows, better grass, fewer mosquitos and other biting insects, magnificent scenery and you can camp above the cloud which tends to persist in the north-facing valleys.

Waymarking on the GR10

FUEL

The three types of camping gas most commonly available are:

- The ones you pierce and have been called the 'original' cylinders.
- The 'easy-clic' resealable cylinders, which is the main resealable system used in Southern Europe.
- Screw-on resealable cylinders, such as those manufactured by Coleman and Primus, are the most widely used in Britain, northern Europe and the USA and have been called 'Coleman-style' gas cylinders.

Where they are mentioned in the text, they were in stock when hiking the route in 2022, but it cannot be guaranteed that they will be in stock when you pass through. 'Coleman-style' cylinders are fairly readily available nowadays, but the locals mainly use the 'original' or 'easy-clic' cylinders and these still have greater availability. Liquid fuels are widely available but make sure you know what you are buying!

WATER

Water can be a problem if it is hot. When walking in temperatures of 25–30°C, you will need at least half a litre (one pint) of water for each hour of walking plus about two litres for a 'dry' camp. This is a guideline and will vary considerably from person to person and will depend on the temperature.

Most towns, villages and hamlets in the Pyrenees have fountains with untreated spring water. The locals and most walkers will drink the water without further treatment. You will often find fountains or 'piped' water as you walk along the trail. It should be obvious whether this water comes from a spring or a surface stream. Spring water is usually of a high quality and can be drunk with confidence. You should be more cautious about surface streams, especially woodland streams or streams in areas which are well stocked with sheep or cattle.

The waterpoints are only shown on the map if they are considered safe to drink without further treatment, however, some hikers will prefer to treat all water using a chemical treatment or filtration. Boiling your water to make it safe to drink only makes sense if you take most of your drinks in the form of tea, coffee or soup.

Eau non potable is widely put on fountains in villages. This generally means that the water has not been treated and likely has not been tested by the authorities. The main reason for the sign is probably the avoidance of any claim for compensation, rather than saying anything about the quality of the water.

SWIMMING

Swimming is often mentioned in this guide. Pyrenean lakes and streams tend to be distinctly chilly and you can expect great blocks of ice to be floating on any lake above 2000m right through to mid June. A swimming costume is not de rigueur for the 'lightweight' backpacker and discreet skinny-dipping seems to be accepted by other users of the mountains. It's normally strictly forbidden to swim in reservoirs.

USING THIS GUIDE

The stages have been organised with the walker who wants to use accommodation in mind. Those who are camping are advised to completely ignore the stages so as to camp well away from towns and villages. There are some stages where those requiring accommodation will have to follow the alternative route rather than the 'main' route.

For a fit walker, it would be possible to complete the trek somewhere in the vicinity of 45 days by combining stages. This would require some planning ahead to ensure daily distances are realistic and accommodation options fit the intended schedule.

The GR10 is very well way-marked with red and white slashes throughout, and in good visibility, when the ground is free of snow, you should have no difficulty following the trail. In the few places where the waymarking is inadequate, or a waymark goes missing, the route description should be used to aid route-finding. The 1:100,000 maps in this guidebook are mainly to give you a feel for the terrain and to help with the planning but they are not detailed enough for fine navigation.

The beautiful Lac d'Anglas is passed on Stage 14

It is recommended that you carry IGN 1:50,000 maps in the mountains because you will need them if you get lost or you want to deviate from the GR10. Detailed maps are essential if you intend following the route in early season, when there could be extensive snowfields. See Appendix C for further information and company websites from where you can purchase these maps.

Most navigational mistakes occur because the walker does not look at the map or guidebook until they are lost! It is much easier to follow the waymarks carefully than to work out what to do if you lose them. The route descriptions and maps in the guide are designed to prevent you getting lost in the first place but will be of little use once you are lost! Keep the guidebook handy, not buried in your rucksack.

The base maps for this guide have been derived from open-source and database information and, as such, have not been subject to the detailed checks that would be applied to a map made by a national mapping agency, but they have been reviewed by the authors.

The terms left and right in the text always refer to left and right of the direction of travel, not the direction of flow of rivers! Places, buildings and other features on the maps that are significant for route navigation are shown in **bold** in the route descriptions. Throughout the route an indication is given of facilities available (accommodation, bothies, campsites, campgrounds, waterpoints, foodshops, picnic sites, tourist offices), and at the end of the stage facilities are listed with their contact details. A facilities summary table can be found in Appendix B.

Maps and apps

The cheapest way to get a complete detailed map of the GR10 is to buy the FFRandonnée TopoGuides which come in four volumes complete with map pages at 1:50,000, www.ffrandonnee.fr

The Pyrenees is covered by the IGN Carte de Randonnée series maps at 1:50,000 (Rando edition). Numbers 1–8, 10 and 11 are required. IGN maps at 1:25,000 are available, but they are not needed.

Maps are available to buy at www.mapsworldwide.com, www.stanfords.co.uk, www.themapshop.co.uk and www.themapcentre.com. Complete IGN 1:25,000 and 1:100,000 coverage of France is available for GPS from Memory-map: www.memory-map.co.uk. OutdoorActive have the 1:100,000 and 1:25,000 IGN maps. The French IGN maps – complete with the GR10 clearly marked on them – are available in digital form through the IGNRando app.

Timings

The timings given in the guide are the actual walking times recorded by the author. These do not include any time for breaks or breathers, and actual walking time will depend on other factors such as group size, navigational ability, fitness, load and conditions. As a guideline, expect to take a total time about 50% longer than the time given, which means allowing nine hours for a six-hour walking day. This will obviously depend on your walking patterns and how you plan your day. Times to climb peaks assume you are fit and walking without a pack.

Distances, ascent and height profiles

Distances don't mean very much on the GR10 where the steepness and roughness of the terrain is far more important than the distance. Distances and ascent have been estimated from the maps. The height profiles are intended to show the general trend of the day's walk and won't show all ups and downs.

GPS

GPX tracks of the GR10 route can be found online to download and use along the route.

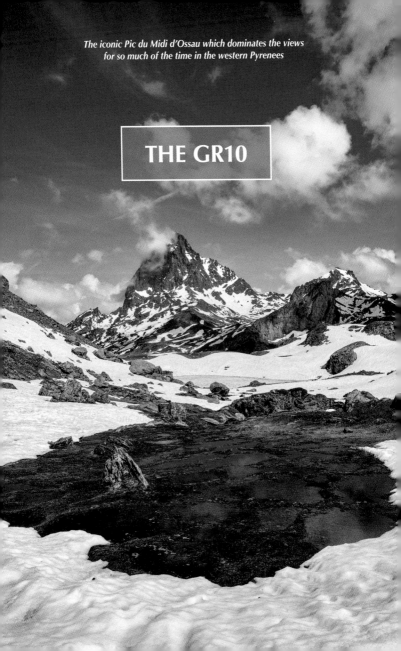

The iconic Pic du Midi d'Ossau which dominates the views for so much of the time in the western Pyrenees

THE GR10

1 HENDAYE-PLAGE TO ETSAUT

KEY INFORMATION

Distance	221km
Total ascent	11,300m
Time	68hr walking
Maps	IGN Carte de Randonnées 1:50,000 maps 1–3

Plateau de Lhers (Stage 12)

The first nine stages to Sainte-Engrâce are over the green rolling hills of the Basque Country. This is followed by a rapid transition to the steep limestone peaks of the High Pyrenees. This is the easiest section of the GR10, but in early season there could be problems with snow in the final stages.

Getting to the start from Hendaye railway station
Head NE from the station, then turn left over the railway and follow the road all the way to the old casino on the seafront at Hendaye-Plage (40mins). If you are on a local train it is quicker to get off at les Deux Jumeaux station and then head N to the seafront (once on the promenade turn left to reach the official start of the GR10).

STAGE 1

Hendaye-Plage to Olhette

Start	Résidence Croisière (old casino), Hendaye-Plage
Distance	21km
Total ascent	1200m
Total descent	1100m
Time	6hr 5min
High point	N slopes of Mandale (530m)
Note	Although Coleman-style camping gas is difficult to find in Hendaye, all types of camping gas are available at the Decathlon store on the Txingudi commercial area at the southwest end of Irún near junction 2 of the A-8 autopista in Spain.

Once Hendaye is left behind the GR10 provides easy walking, through a mixture of woodland and pasture, over the steep rolling hills of the Basque Country.

The old 'casino' in Hendaye-Plage

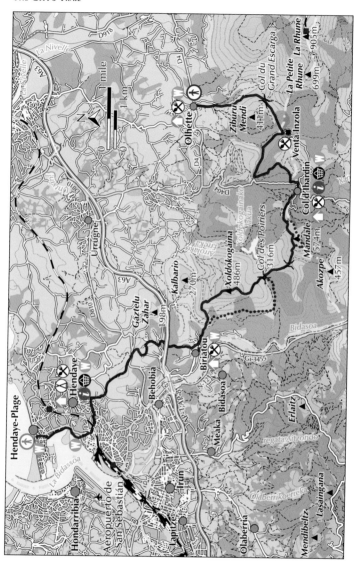

Hendaye has the international railway station and the main shopping areas while the beach resort of Hendaye-Plage, with its 3km sandy beach, has most of the accommodation and tourist facilities. There are toilets just along the seafront to the W of the start.

The town of Hendaye is only separated from the Spanish town of Irún by the Bidassoa river. The GR10 starts at the Résidence Croisière on the seafront. ▶ For those who are travelling light, the E end of the beach is costumes-optional.

Head S down the Boulevard du Général Leclerc and, at a large roundabout, veer right down Rue des Citronniers to reach la Baie de Chingoudy. Turn left along the promenade, passing two sets of toilets and a waterpoint by a play area, to reach the Stade Bixente Lizarazu football ground. Veer left round the far end of the pitch, pass another waterpoint and go under the bridge to a roundabout. Keep straight on along a passage between flats and veer left up a minor road and along a footpath to another roundabout. Keep straight on up the Chemin de Biaténia which merges with the Boulevard de l'Emperor (30min). Turn right here if you need the large Intermarché supermarket (15min), which sells original and easy-clic camping gas.

Turn left for the GR10 and fork right up Rue Errondenia. At the top of the road turn right up the Rue

This magnificent building, built in 1885 in neo-Moorish style, was originally a casino but is now occupied by a selection of restaurants and tourist shops.

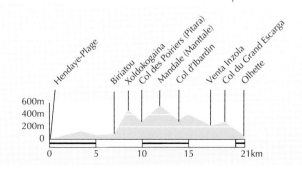

de Pausoa and out of town. At the top of the hill turn left down a track, soon forking right and right again for your first wild camping opportunity (50min). Fork left to the top of Migeltxoenborda (132m) and veer left down to the **D810** road (formerly N10). Turn left along the road and, after 100m, fork right down a track which soon becomes a path. At a junction, fork right along a track which becomes a small tarmac road. Then it's left at a junction, fork right at the top of a hill, straight on at the next junction, sharp left, left again and next right to reach a tunnel which takes you under the **A63 motorway**. Ignore a sharp left turn and some tarmac drives to reach a junction at the top of the hill (1hr 40min).

> Turn right if you want to visit the hamlet of Biriatou. There is a waterpoint in the hotel car park and public toilets with waterpoint near the auberge, below the church. If you visit Biriatou you can rejoin the GR10 by following the signs rather than returning to the junction.

In bad weather the old GR10 route is preferable, following the track traversing S to a 4-way junction. Take the right-hand of the two left turns and climb to rejoin the GR10 at Col de Poiriers (Pitara).

Turn left for the GR10, then fork right, turn left, fork right and climb. As the gradient eases, fork right and immediately left up a track (1hr 50min). Right and left forks bring you under powerlines. ◄

The GR10 goes left and immediately right to follow a path which climbs to the right of the powerlines before reaching a viewpoint, with a picnic table, under the powerlines at the foot of the rocky NW ridge of Xoldokogaina. After crossing the ridge, fork right, right again and then turn right to regain the ridge above the crags. Follow the path easily up to the monument on the summit of **Xoldokogaina** (2hr 55min, 486m).

Descend roughly S to the Col d'Osin, veering left along a better track to the **Col des Poiriers**, which has good dry campsites and an ancient tumulus (3hr 15min, 316m). Follow the path, roughly SE, which climbs into the forest and reaches Col des Joncs (419m). Veer left up the ridge, fork right then turn sharp left back onto the ridge and turn right up the ridge.

The remains of an old hill fort, **Redoute de la Baïonette**, are worth visiting in good weather. They are reached by taking a sharp right turn onto the ridge and then following a good path northeast to the summit of Mandale. The remains are found at borderstone 9. After borderstone 10 veer slightly left to rejoin the GR10 for the descent to the Col d'Ibardin.

The GR10 contours the N slopes of **Mandale** (574m). ▶ Eventually, at a switchback, turn right down a small path to reach Elizalde Restaurante at the **Col d'Ibardin** (4hr 5min).

The mountain ahead with the communications mast is la Rhune (905m).

A stream below Col d'Ibardin

The Col d'Ibardin has a multitude of bar-restaurants and supermarkets offering food and alcohol at Spanish prices. The Elizalde Restaurante offers accommodation. There are public toilets with water at the garage and a tourist office across the road.

Follow the road, which is the border between France and Spain, down to the actual col (317m). Turn left at the roundabout, down the **D404**. You soon fork right up a path, the Sentier des Mulets, turning right just before a gate and climbing steeply before veering right and turning left to descend on an increasingly good track to a barrier. Fork right along a path and turn right just before returning to the D404 (4hr 45min). Descend through woods to the left of a stream and eventually, just after a log bridge, turn right across the stream and follow another stream gently uphill. Stay on the right-hand side of the stream at a log bridge. ◀ Enter Spain at borderstone 18 to arrive at **Venta Inzola** (5hr 15min, 115m) which is a bar-restaurant.

You are on a Roman road originally built to serve the mining industry.

Cross the stream immediately N of the Venta and follow the path as it climbs through the woods back into France to reach a complex junction at the **Col du Grand Escarga** (Deskargahandiko Lepoa) (5hr 35min, 273m). This col provides the last obvious campsites before Olhette. Follow the right-hand of the two paths, which goes straight on, veering left as it descends gently before forking left on a smaller path. After another left fork you arrive at the roadhead at **Olhette** (6hr 5min, 65m).

Olhette is an attractive hamlet with gîtes d'étape and hotel accommodation. The Manttu-Baïta has lovely rooms in a fine old Basque farmhouse at the roadhead and the Gîte d'étape Trapero Baïta is on the 'main' road about 500m further N. There is a waterpoint at the Gîte d'étape Manttu-Baïta.

FACILITIES FOR STAGE 1

Hendaye

Hendaye tourist office, east of the old casino: tel 05 59 20 00 34, www.hendaye-tourisme.fr

Camping des Deux Jumeaux, along the coast road near the east end of Hendaye-Plage: tel 05 59 20 01 65, www.camping-des-2Jumeaux.com

Accommodation close to the railway station:

Hôtel de la Gare: tel 05 59 20 81 90, http://saintmartinmaite.pagesperso-orange.fr

Biriatou

Hôtel-restaurant les Jardins de Bakea: tel 05 59 20 02 01, www.bakea.fr

Auberge Hiribarren, chambres d'hôtes with bar-restaurant: tel 05 59 29 96 77, www.aubergehiribarren.fr

Col d'Ibardin

Elizalde Restaurante offers accommodation: tel 0948 631 024 (Spanish)

Olhette

Manttu-Baïta, high-quality chambres d'hôtes accommodation, spa and pool: tel 05 59 54 46 72 or 06 20 43 49 25, www.chambre-d-hote-cote-basque-manttu.fr

Gîte d'étape Trapero Baïta, accommodation, meals, a swimming pool and possibly camping in the garden. English spoken: tel 05 59 54 42 596

Hôtel-restaurant Trabenia: tel 06 23 58 58 84, www.hotel-trabenia.com

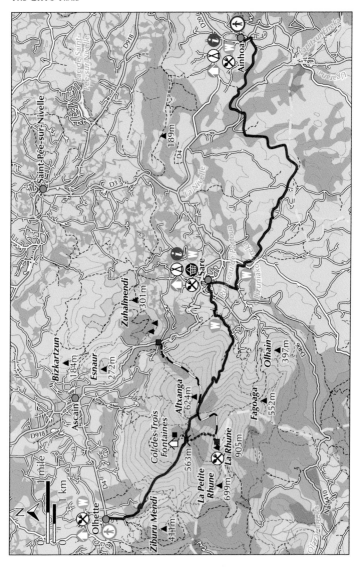

STAGE 2

Olhette to Ainhoa

Start	Olhette
Distance	21km
Total ascent	700m
Total descent	700m
Time	5hr 25min
High point	Col des Trois Fontaines (563m)

The stage starts with an easy climb to the Col des Trois Fontaines (Errepausuko Lepoa) from where it would be possible to climb la Rhune (905m), with its communication masts and station. There is too much road walking after Sare, though the scenery is still delightful. The profile may look flat, but it is actually a succession of small ups and downs; don't expect flat walking in the Basque Country!

From Olhette return to the roadhead, cross the stream, pass through the car park and take the path from the far left corner. You soon fork left, ignore turns to left and right, fork left again and turn right along a better track. Ignore assorted small paths and climb steadily until you fork left up a faint path immediately below the Col des Trois Fontaines.

The summit of **la Rhune**, which is widely considered to be the first proper mountain of the Pyrenees and is an icon of the Basque Country, can be reached by following the main path, which veers right to gain the west ridge of la Rhune. Climb to the top by following the green arrows on a popular path. There are communications masts, a minature railway station, several bar-restaurants and tourist shops marring the summit, but the views toward the coast are sensational. It will take 1½ hours to get there and back.

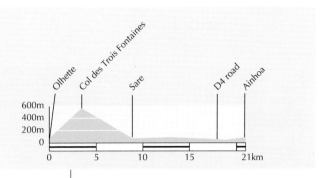

The GR10 continues to the col (1hr 30min, 563m). There is a small bothy, Arranoxola, about 300m N of the col.

On the descent you cross a number of streams of dubious quality. Head E along the right-hand path, veering right, roughly SE, to reach the rack railway which takes tourists from the Col de St-Ignace (NW of Sare) to the summit of la Rhune. Cross the **railway track** and follow the path, which descends gently to the right of the track. Turn sharp right at the second group of ruined farm buildings, then left after crossing a small stream. The track gradually improves before becoming a small tarmac road. Pass a waterpoint, turn sharp left at a farm and then down a path to the left of a house. Pass another waterpoint before turning right along a small road, which you follow down to the main road. Go half-left through the car park and right up a path, passing a large fronton, swimming pool and small supermarket to arrive at the church at the centre of **Sare** (2hr 45min, 70m).

A fronton is the court for playing **pelota** – a Basque sport bearing some similarity to the game of squash. There are many variations to pelota, played with a ball and using one's hand, a racket, a wooden bat or a basket, usually played by teams of two.

Sare is a small village with a tourist office, campground and many small shops. Public toilets and

The cobbled path leaving Sare

a waterpoint are by the swimming pool. Hôtels Arraya and Lastiry are in the centre of the village, with cheaper accommodation further along the GR10. There is a bus service from Sare connecting with the rail network at St-Jean-de-Luz.

Turn right after the church. The road leads to a cobbled lane heading out of the village. Keep straight on up a tarmac road and up some steps to reach a road (3hr). Turn right for the Hôtel Pikassaria and Camping la Petite Rhune, which has a gîte d'étape.

The GR10 goes sharp left. Ignore several turns and keep straight on down a track, then turn right along a cobbled path. Pass a waterpoint before turning right along the D306. Almost immediately turn left across the river and veer left up a track at the end of the road. Turn right along a minor road and then fork left. Continue until a track forks left at Bordaberriko Borda. Follow this track which becomes a small road. Fork left, then go straight on down a track at a road junction. Turn left at a track junction and follow the **border** past borderstone 63. Cut left down a path, soon to rejoin the track. Cross a stream, then shortly afterwards turn left and follow a path along the stream. The path leaves the stream and crosses the track before joining a major track. Follow this alongside a large stream, cross the **D4** road and follow a smaller track. Eventually turn left across a bridge and the track soon becomes a path. Ignore any right turns and follow the path as it climbs to join a small tarmac road. Ignore a sharp right turn to Dancharia and arrive at **Ainhoa**. Veer left to reach the tourist office, which is in the mairie opposite the church (5hr 25min, 120m).

Ainhoa is a picture-postcard pretty Basque village of red and white houses. There are several hotels and a campground with a gîte d'étape as well restaurants and several small shops selling Basque linens and souvenirs. There isn't much in the way of supermarkets but bread, cheese and Basque specialities are available. There are toilets, with water, just down the lane from the tourist office. There is more accommodation at Dancharia, about 3km SSW of Ainhoa.

FACILITIES FOR STAGE 2

Sare

Tourist office: tel 05 59 54 20 14, www.sare.fr

Hôtel Arraya: tel 05 59 54 20 46, www.arraya.com

Hôtel-restaurant Lastiry: tel 05 59 22 24 30, www.hotel-lastiry-sare.com/fr

Hôtel-restaurant Pikassaria: tel 05 59 54 21 51, www.hotel-pikassaria.com

Camping la Petite Rhune, 300m from the GR10, also has a gîte d'étape. No meals but nearby bar-restaurant: tel 05 59 54 23 97, www.lapetiterhune.com

Ainhoa

Tourist office: tel 05 59 29 93 99, www.ainhoa.fr

Camping Harazpy, also has a gîte d'étape. No meals: tel 05 59 29 89 38, www.camping-harazpy.com

Hôtel la Maison Oppoca, recently renovated and very enticing: tel 05 59 29 90 72, www.oppoca.com

Hôtel Argi Eder, has a renowned gourmet restaurant: tel 05 59 93 72 00, www.argi-eder.com

Hôtel Ithurria, the choice place to splash out on luxury and has a superb gourmet restaurant: tel 05 59 29 92 11, www.ithurria.com

STAGE 3
Ainhoa to Bidarray

Start	Ainhoa
Distance	21km
Total ascent	800m
Total descent	800m
Time	5hr 45min
High point	Col des Trois-Croix (510m), Col de Méhatché (716m)

Wild camping is possible throughout this stage, which follows exposed grassy ridges typical of the Basque Country. The GR10 contours round most of the summits but, in good weather, you may prefer to take in up to four summits: Errebi, Atxulegi, Mont Bizkayluze and Gorospil. The descent to Bidarray is down an exposed, rocky mountain path that could take a long time for the inexperienced or overladen hiker, especially in bad weather. This is the most difficult descent on the GR10.

Follow the lane right, E, past the tourist office, veering left and right before turning right at a junction with a waterpoint and forking left up a dirt road. Climb steeply, passing nine large white crosses and a shrine with a waterpoint (running

51

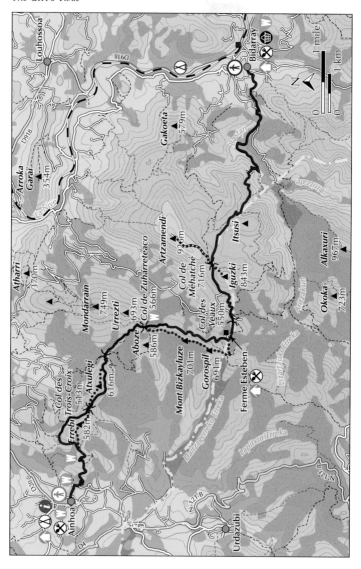

'Crucifiction of Christ' at Chapelle de l'Aubépine

well in summer 2022) before reaching the Chapelle de l'Aubépine (40min, 389m). Here there are a multitude of small stone crosses and three large white crosses depicting the crucifiction of Christ. ▶ Veer left past the crosses.

This is not the Col des Trois-Croix!

In good weather you may prefer to take the obvious path over the summit of **Errebi** (582m), rejoining the GR10 at the Col des Trois-Croix (same timing).

The GR10 passes old mine workings as it contours round the N slopes of Errebi. Shortly after a right fork, turn

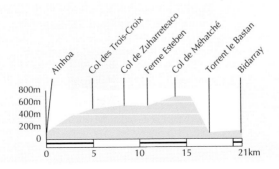

right up a path and soon resume contouring, passing a barn and merging with a small track. Climb to a shallow col where you resume contouring on a bigger track before climbing gently to the **Col des Trois-Croix** (1hr 20min, 510m), which is marked by a single small iron cross!

You could traverse **Atxulegi** (617m) (taking about 15min longer) but the GR10 continues along the track round the S slopes, descending gently to an unnamed col with a complex junction. Head SE along the middle of the three tracks to another shallow col and continue on the track that veers right and climbs gently to the **Col de Zuharreteaco** (2hr 10min, 566m) with a spring that is often dry by mid-summer.

> In good weather it would be preferable to follow the ridge, roughly south, over **Mont Bizkayluze** (701m) and **Gorospil** (691m) to reach the border before turning left to regain the GR10 at Ferme Esteben.

The GR10 follows the track contouring the E side of the ridge. The track has become a path by the time you fork left as the end of the ridge is approached, then descends gently to reach a concrete track. Turn left and pass the back entrance to **Ferme Esteben** (2hr 50min, 580m), which used to offer accommodation and meals but is now sadly closed.

The GR10 continues down the concrete track and goes straight on along a fence, when the track veers right. This path passes borderstone 77 and soon joins the tarmac access road to Ferme Esteben. Follow this road to a junction at the **Col des Veaux** (550m). There is a sign to Venta Burkaitz with bar-restaurant and accommodation, in Spain, which is about 300m S of the Col des Veaux.

In good weather you might like to climb the grassy Pic Iguzki (843m) to the E, regaining the GR10 at the Col de Méhatché.

The GR10 goes straight on up a track then follows the main track left at a junction and forks right up a path, veering left at the top of the fence to reach a tarmac road. ◄ The GR10 follows the road right along the N slopes of the hill to reach the **Col de Méhatché** (3hr 35min, 716m).

From the Col de Méhatché you could climb **Artzamendi** (926m), following the tarmac road to the communications complex on the summit, or **Pic Iguzki** (844m) by its grassy northeast ridge.

The GR10 turns half-right, E, to reach a ridge which is followed past borderstone 82 and on to borderstone 83 at the Col d'Artzatey. Skirt left of the next top to the next col (3hr 55min, 630m). Before reaching the barn on the col, turn sharp right and descend steeply into a crag-bound valley. A rough rocky path then descends down the N slopes of the valley. ▶ Look out for the huge griffon vultures who nest in surrounding cliff faces.

There are now wires to protect the most exposed rocksteps.

Towards the bottom of the descent a small path goes steeply up to the left to the **Grotte le Saint-que-Sue** (Harpeko Saindua). Legend suggests that a young shepherdess was found 'petrified' in the rock. The cave became a shrine and site of pilgrimage with claims that the 'holy water' oozing through the cave would cure skin and eye diseases.

Eventually the path reaches a road (4hr 45min). Turn left along it before descending via switchbacks to cross a bridge over **Torrent le Bastan**. Follow the road along or above the S bank of the river, passing a few swimming holes. About 20m before the road recrosses the river (5hr 20min), turn right up a steep path, then left along an old track. Fork right and then veer right round a ridge to reach a road by Gîte Urrizate. Follow the road, ignoring a sharp left turn, to arrive at the W end of Bidarray (5hr 45min, 150m). ▶ Head E down the road into **Bidarray** (5hr 45min, 150m).

If you don't need the facilities at Bidarray you could turn right here and start Stage 4.

The main facilities for walkers are in the upper village where there is a small shop in the bar-restaurant Iparla complex and the Hôtel Barberaenea. There is a waterpoint outside the church as well as public toilets and further waterpoints in the churchyard. Bidarray is on the railway line between Bayonne and Saint-Jean-Pied-de-Port. The station and the Hôtel Noblia are in the lower village beside the river. Camping Amestoya is also on the D918, about 2km N of Bidarray.

FACILITIES FOR STAGE 3

Col des Veaux

Ferme Esteben bar-restaurant and gîte d'étape: tel 05 59 29 82 72, www.gites-refuges.com/v2/detail-1868.htm

Bidarray

Hôtel Barberaenea: tel 05 59 37 74 86, www.hotel-bidarray.com

Hôtel-restaurant Noblia: tel 05 59 37 70 89, www.logishotels.com

Camping Amestoya: tel 05 59 37 25 81, www.camping-bidarray.fr

Arteka adventure school, offers accommodation to hikers if not fully booked: tel 05 59 37 71 34, www.arteka-eh.com

Gîte d'étape Aire Zabal is in the upper village: tel 07 50 04 11 61, www.giteairezabal.fr

STAGE 4
Bidarray to Saint-Étienne-de-Baïgorry

Start	Bidarray
Distance	16km
Total ascent	1300m
Total descent	1300m
Time	6hr 15min
High point	Pic d'Iparla (1044m), Buztanzelhay (1029m)

The GR10 follows the magnificent border ridge over the Crête d'Iparla, reaching 1000m for the first time, before descending to Saint-Étienne-de-Baïgorry. It's arguably the most impressive part of the trail in the Basque Country. It's probably best to assume there will be no available water until well down the descent to Saint-Étienne-de-Baïgorry. There are good, but exposed, campsites throughout the section. Don't attempt to camp actually on the crête (ridge) if there is any risk of a thunderstorm.

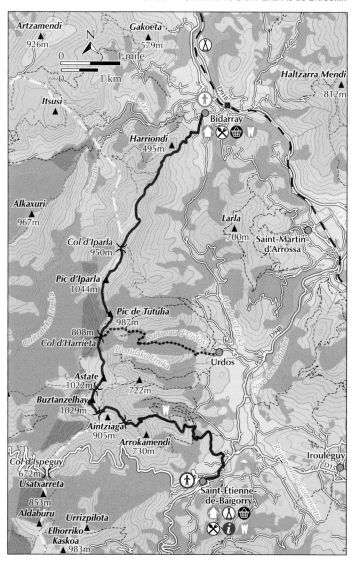

Pic d'Iparla, the first 1000m peak on the GR10

If ice or snow lies on the main trail then take this alternate trail which loops safely around the back of Iparla before climbing up to the edge of the ridge.

The GR10 trail leaving Bidarray is a little confusing as it has recently been slightly re-routed but old GR10 way markers still mark the former route. In reality it makes no difference which one you take as they both quickly meet up and once on the trail to Iparla you can't easily go wrong. Follow the road SSW from the W end of Bidarray, forking right then taking the second right to reach the roadhead at Urdabordia. Follow the track to the right of the farm and veer left, past a gate and then follow the path between wire fencing to reach the ridge. Follow the path up the ridge to a junction at a saddle (1hr). Ignore the path going right ◄ and continue climbing fairly easily up the ridge on a rocky path, skirting left of the upper crags. The path now climbs gently up grassy slopes, veering left to Point 905. Continue along the edge of the steep escarpment. After the **Col d'Iparla** (2hr 20min, 950m) the path becomes rougher, passing borderstone 90 before the final climb to the summit of **Pic d'Iparla**, marked by a concrete pillar (2hr 45min, 1044m). You are now stood with a sheer drop in front of you and a magnificent view over the gently rolling Basque farmland below.

Continue along the ridge over two minor tops and descend gently on a rough path to the Col de Gapelu and over another minor summit, **Pic de Tutulia** (983m), and SW down to **Col d'Harrieta** (3hr 35min, 808m), which is easily identified by the trees that cross the ridge. There is a waterpoint signed along a path 400m SSW from the col, but the water looks as if it needs filtering and the reliability of the spring is questionable. ▶

Climb the ridge ahead, through the woods, skirting crags. Once out of the woods, the path climbs gently up the grassy ridge to a tiny cairn on **Astate** (4hr 15min, 1022m). Veer slightly right, following the ridge to descend to a col with the remains of an ancient burial mound and climb to the large summit cairn on **Buztanzelhay** (4hr 35min, 1029m). The path initially descends SW to avoid crags, before veering SE to the Col de Buztanzelhay (843m). The GR10 forks left and descends steeply before veering right and contouring to a col (5hr 10min, 750m) on the E ridge of **Aintziaga** (905m). Cross the ridge and follow the path on the right flank before regaining the ridge at the head of a tarmac track.

Follow this track, shortcutting a couple of switchbacks on the right, pass a reliable waterpoint and fork right on a path along the ridge top, just before the track

In bad weather there is an escape route signed E from the col down to Urdos from where you can follow roads to Saint-Étienne-de-Baïgorry.

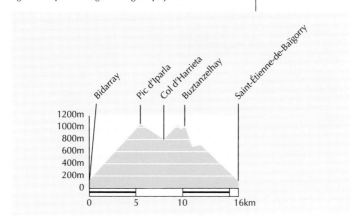

descends left. Eventually the path veers sharp left at a shooting butt and descends to a narrow road (5hr 50min). Turn right and then fork left down a path which shortcuts switchbacks in the road. On regaining the road, fork right and continue down, passing the holiday village VVF. Turn right at the gendarmerie to arrive at the **D948** road in **Saint-Étienne-de-Baïgorry**.

There is a bar-restaurant, toilets, pizzeria and tourist office where you reach the D948. Turn left and then right up the Saint-Jean-Pied-de-Port road for the campground and the Intermarché supermarket, which stocks original and easy-clic camping gas.

The GR10 goes right to cross la Nive des Aldudes (6hr 15min, 162m). If you don't need the facilities in the village you could turn left here to start Stage 5.

Turn right, W, along the river for a public park with water, toilets and picnic tables, the Spar supermarket, Gîte Gaineko Karrikan and the hotels. There is a bus service to Saint-Jean-Pied-de-Port.

FACILITIES FOR STAGE 4

Saint-Étienne-de-Baïgorry

Tourist office: tel 05 59 37 47 28, www.pyrenees-basques.com

Gîte Gaineko Karrikan, chambres d'hôtes, gîte d'étape and meals: tel 06 70 01 15 54

Villages VVF Iparla, aimed at tourists but will take GR10 hikers: tel 05 59 37 40 58, www.vvf-villages.fr

Camping Municipal Irouleguy: tel 05 59 37 43 96

Hôtel-restaurant Arce, a beautiful up-market hotel: tel 05 59 37 40 14, www.hotel-arce.com

Hôtel-restaurant Juantorena: tel 05 59 37 40 78, www.hotelrestaurantjuantorena.fr

STAGE 5

Saint-Étienne-de-Baïgorry to Saint-Jean-Pied-de-Port

Start	Saint-Étienne-de-Baïgorry
Distance	20km
Total ascent	900m
Total descent	900m
Time	5hr 5min
High point	Munhoa (1021m)

Much of the walking in this section is on farm roads or tracks. If the weather is fine, climbing up Oylarandoy is well worth it. In bad weather you may prefer to follow the road to the west of Oylarandoy and continue along it until you reach the east ridge of Munhoa. There are several waterpoints on the route and exposed camping is possible on the ridges.

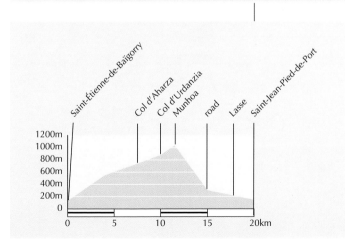

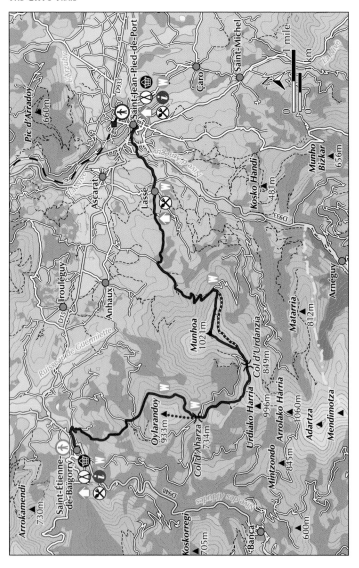

From the bridge over la Nive des Aldudes head E along a narrow road. Pass under the dismantled railway and immediately turn right and climb. Fork right after the second switchback and then fork left up a track to the left of a farm building. Keep straight on up a path at a junction and veer left when you meet a track. Ignore two left turns. The first campsites on the ascent are on the left by a third left turn (55min). Continue until you reach a narrow tarmac road, then turn right to a road junction (561m). Keep straight on up a track, then fork left and continue until the track levels off on the NE ridge of **Oylarandoy**.

> If you have surplus energy you can climb this ridge to the **summit of Oylarandoy** (933m) where a hermitage was first built in 1706. The shrine has been rebuilt on several occasions and the latest (1985) rebuild even includes stained-glass windows. You could then rejoin the GR10 down the gentler south ridge. The steep bracken-covered northeast ridge is not recommended and it would be easier to follow the GR10 to the Col d'Aharza and climb the south ridge from there (up and down in 35min).

A traverse of the east slopes of Oylarandoy

The GR10 veers S below a cabin and soon passes a small barn with a waterpoint (running summer 2022). There follows a gently rising traverse of the SE slopes of Oylarandoy to arrive at the road at the **Col d'Aharza** (1hr 55min, 734m) where there is a waterpoint at the SE corner of the sheepfold (running summer 2022).

Turn left along the road and fork right up a farm road. At the high point of this road turn left down a small path to the Col de Leizarze (828m) and follow the path as it veers and climbs to a road just below a large barn on the E ridge of Urdiakoharria. Turn left down the road to reach the **Col d'Urdanzia** (2hr 45min, 849m). Follow the road forking right up the ridge. When the road crosses the ridge at a shallow saddle, fork left and climb the grassy ridge to a small communications mast on the summit of **Munhoa** (3hr 15min, 1021m). ◄

In bad weather you may prefer to follow the road along the S slopes of Munhoa.

From the summit descend to the right of the fence to return to the road. Keep straight on at a junction, but stay on the ridge when the road descends right. Continue down the ridge, then turn left at a road before shortcutting to a cattle trough with a waterpoint (3hr 35min, 750m). Follow the track that goes diagonally left, NW, zigzagging down the hillside. ◄ The last good campsite before Saint-Jean-Pied-de-Port is on a spur on your right about half way down. Continue down to a tarmac farm road (4hr 5min) and turn left. Turn right, then left, fork right and pass a waterpoint outside a farm. Then it's second left and right to the Auberge Etchoinia in the centre of **Lasse** (4hr 35min, 204m) where there are also public toilets with a hot shower.

You may prefer to shortcut down the small paths through the bracken.

Keep straight on and follow the main road to reach a church and fronton, with public toilets, just outside Saint-Jean-Pied-de-Port. Veer right past a waterpoint. The Lidl supermarket is on the main road on your left. Continue down to the busy D918 and follow it SE to a mini-roundabout in **Saint-Jean-Pied-de-Port** (5hr 5min, 170m).

Saint-Jean-Pied-de-Port is the biggest tourist town in the Basque interior. Turn left for the tourist office and Carrefour supermarket, which is on the D933 heading E. Beside the supermarket is Maya Sport which stocks walking equipment and all types of camping gas. Turn right, S, for the municipal campground. Saint-Jean-Pied-de-Port is the main starting point for the principal Camino de Santiago pilgrimage trail and has a range of accommodation to suit the pilgrims on that trail as well as a wide range of hotels, bar-restaurants and shops. Only a small selection of the available accommodation is listed below. There is a railway station which links to the main French rail system via Bayonne.

FACILITIES FOR STAGE 5

Lasse

Auberge Etchoinia, accommodation and bar-restaurant: tel 05 59 37 01 57, www.auberge-etchoinia-pays-basque.com

Saint-Jean-Pied-de-Port

Tourist office: tel 05 59 37 03 57, www.saintjeanpieddeport-paysbasque-tourisme.com

Gîte d'étape Compostella: tel 05 59 37 02 36

Gîte d'étape Ultreïa: tel 06 80 88 46 22, www.ultreia64.fr

Camping Municipal Plaza Berri, enquire at the tourist office: tel 05 59 37 03 57

Hôtel Les Remparts: tel 05 59 37 13 79, www.hoteldesremparts.fr

Hôtel Central: tel 05 59 37 00 22, www.centralhotel64.com

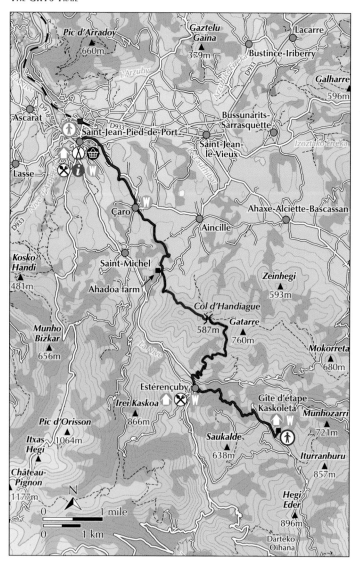

STAGE 6
Saint-Jean-Pied-de-Port to Gîte d'étape Kaskoleta

Start	Saint-Jean-Pied-de-Port
Distance	17km
Total ascent	900m
Total descent	400m
Time	4hr 55min
High point	Col d'Handiague (587m), Gîte d'étape Kaskoleta (615m)

This is an easy stage with a road walk followed by a crossing of Handiamendi (642m) and then a road walk to the Gîte d'étape Kaskoleta. Although we would normally recommend pushing on from Estérençuby village to the gîte d'étape so as to avoid a punishing stage 7, at the time of writing the gîte d'étape closed for major renovations and so unless you're equipped for camping then you'll have to stay back in Estérençuby.

From the mini-roundabout, keep straight on down Rue d'Uhart. Turn left at the end, across a bridge and under an arch into the 'old town'. Keep straight on up the cobbled street. This street has waterpoints, gîtes d'étape and shops

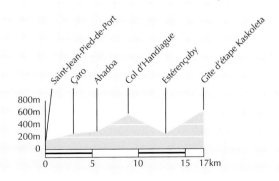

Early morning mist on the ascent of Handiamendi

specialising in supporting Camino de Santiago walkers. La Boutique du Pèlerin sells Coleman-style gas cylinders.

> The **Camino de Santiago** is the name of any of the pilgrimage routes, from all over Europe, to the shrine of the Apostle St James (St Jacques in French, or St Iago in Spanish), in Santiago de Compostela in orthwest Spain, where tradition has it that the remains of the saint are buried.

Exit the old town under the arch of la Porte Saint-Jacques. Keep straight on at the first junction, then veer right on the road to Çaro. Fork right shortly after the road sign indicating the end of town and follow the back road to Çaro. Pass a waterpoint as you rejoin the main road (40min). Almost immediately turn left and fork right to pass through **Çaro** and keep straight on at the end of the village. Ignore two left turns and eventually fork right down a muddy track into woods. This becomes a path by the time it crosses a stream (poor campsites) and climbs out the other side to reach a road at **Ahadoa farm** (1hr 20min). Turn left, then right and immediately left through a gate and up a track to climb onto open hillside. As the track fades away veer sharp left to a gate and climb to the right of the fence. Here you will find your first good campsites since Saint-Jean-Pied-de-Port. At the top of the fence veer right to a path that climbs diagonally up the NW ridge of Handiamendi, to reach a point just above the **Col d'Handiague** (587m). Veer right and left to reach the farm road at the col (2hr).

Turn right. The road soon becomes a farm track, which contours before starting the descent shortly after a right fork. Ignore sharp left and right turns as the track zigzags down the ridge. The track becomes a tarmac road shortly before reaching the D301. Turn left to the centre of the hamlet of **Estérençuby** (3hr 45min, 231m). There are public toilets with water opposite the Auberge Carricaburu and the Hôtel Andreinia, with a gîte d'étape, is just up the road.

Follow the road steeply up to the right of the church, ignoring right, right and left turns. Keep left at the fourth junction, then turn sharp right up a tarmac drive and follow the path to the left of two houses. Turn right when you reach the road and go straight on at a junction before forking left. Ignore a left turn before reaching the drive for the **Gîte d'étape Kaskoleta** (4hr 55min, 615m), which is set back from the road on the left. There is a waterpoint at the entrance to the gîte. At the time of writing the gîte was closed for major renovations. Check beforehand that it's re-opened otherwise you'll either have to camp or stay an hour back down the trail in Estérençuby.

FACILITIES FOR STAGE 6

Estérençuby

Hôtel Andreinia, hotel and gîte d'étape: tel 05 59 37 09 70, www.hotel-andreinia.com

Hôtel Auberge Carricaburu, accommodation and bar-restaurant: tel 05 59 37 09 77

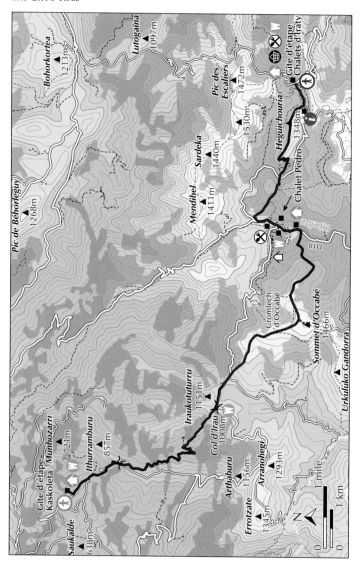

STAGE 7

*Gîte d'étape Kaskoleta to Gîte
d'étape Chalets d'Iraty*

Start	Gîte d'étape Kaskoleta
Distance	20km
Total ascent	1400m
Total descent	700m
Time	6hr 20min
High point	Col on Ithurramburu (820m), Sommet d'Occabé (1456m), Heguichouria (1348m)

The main feature of this stage is the easy but exposed traverse of the Sommet d'Occabé. Camping is possible throughout the stage. It is a very long day if you start from Estérençuby rather than the Gîte d'étape Kaskoleta.

Continue along the road before forking left. After a road joins from back left, the GR10 climbs a steep grass slope on the left to shortcut the switchbacks in the road. Continue up the road until the GR10 keeps straight on up a grassy track at another switchback in the road. Veer slightly left at a five-way junction and cross the road, keeping straight on along a track at another five-way junction at a col on the SSW ridge of **Ithurramburu** (35min, 820m). The track descends gently and eventually crosses two woodland streams (1hr 15min). The second stream is easier to access (the water should be treated before drinking). ▸

About 100m upstream a small water chute is good for a refreshing bathe.

A few minutes later, as the track swings right, turn right up a steep path which heads up the ridge and then follows a steadily rising traverse of the S slopes of the W ridge of **Iraukotuturru** to arrive at a road col (2hr 15min). There is a waterpoint at the farm buildings on the right.

Follow the D301 left to the **Col d'Irau** (1008m). There is a waterpoint by the shepherd's cabins on the left where you may be able to buy cheese. Continue to a road junction by another set of farm buildings. The GR10 continues straight up the grassy slopes ahead. Care will be needed following the waymarks in mist as the path is rather indistinct. Veer left at a GR10 marker stone on the ridge (2hr 55min) and follow a clearer grass track which veers right and soon passes S of the summit of Top 1307. Continue to a junction with the GRT9 (3hr 30min) in an area with at least 15 ancient burial mounds and associated stone circles dating back 4000–5000 years, collectively known as the **Cromlech d'Occabé**.

The actual summit is an undistinguished point (1466m) about 250m further S.

The GR10 continues straight ahead before veering slightly left to pass 150m left of the summit tor on the **Sommet d'Occabé** (3hr 40min). ◄

Descend roughly ENE to a col where the woods encroach on the ridge. The beech forests around Iraty are some of the largest and most beautiful in the Pyrenees though the lion's share are on the Spanish side. Keep straight on, then fork right along the main track and descend easily, ignoring numerous side turns to reach

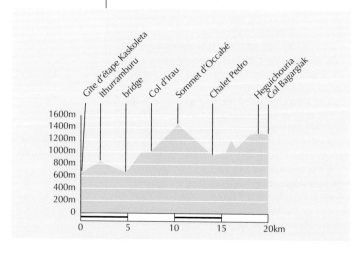

the **D18** road (4hr 25min). Turn left, pass **Chalet Pedro** (1000m) and continue along the road. You will pass a large bothy with toilets, shower, waterpoint and a parking area for motor homes with a bar-restaurant set back from the road on the left. Cross the river, pass a small reservoir and fork right up a road signed to Irati (4hr 40min).

After 100m turn sharp right up a track, zigzag up to the woods and continue climbing, ignoring all turns, to reach a saddle (5hr 10min). Descend the other side and cross the road, passing left of the small reservoir. Follow the track which zigzags up through the woods, ignoring all sideturns, to reach the crest of the ridge and then follow the track along the ridge to the first chalets of the Iraty cross-country ski complex on the summit of **Heguichouria** (1348m). Follow the track to a car park (6hr 10min). The building across the road contains the reception for the gîte d'étape as well as a café, information centre and toilets. Continue left along the road to the

The gîte d'étape Chalets d'Iraty

73

main complex of **Gîte d'étape Chalets d'Iraty** at the Col Bagargiak (6hr 20min, 1327m).

There is a bar-restaurant and a small shop that sells Coleman-style camping gas. The gîte d'étape with toilets and water is behind the tennis courts.

FACILITIES FOR STAGE 7

Chalet Pedro, aimed at holiday and weekend bookings. Booking is recommended for the restaurant: tel 05 59 28 55 98, www.chaletpedro.com

Gîte d'étape Chalets d'Iraty: tel 05 59 28 51 29, www.chalets-iraty.com

STAGE 8
Gîte d'étape Chalets d'Iraty to Logibar

Start	Gîte d'étape Chalets d'Iraty
Distance	17km
Total ascent	500m
Total descent	1400m
Time	5hr
High point	W ridge, Pic des Escaliers (1423m)

Other guides suggest a bad weather alternative descent to Logibar via Larrau, however, the route is unmarked and difficult to follow in good weather. It isn't recommended unless you want to road walk all the way to Logibar. A more sensible bad weather route, avoiding the Pic des Escaliers, is to follow the road traversing the SE slopes of this mountain and then regain the GR10 on Crête Ugatzé. The GR10 doesn't visit the summit of Pic des Escaliers but, in good weather, most walkers will. Some of the paths on the descent to Logibar are rather nebulous.

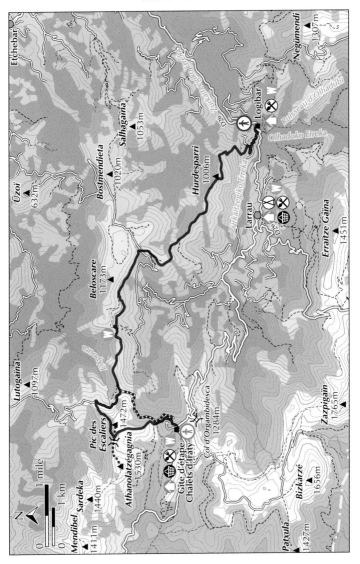

Continue a few metres down the hill then turn left along a minor road. At a switchback in the road, turn left along a good track. Veer right off the track at a junction and follow a path that climbs diagonally right. The path levels off on the grassy S ridge of Pic des Escaliers and then climbs slightly before veering left for a rising traverse to a small grassy saddle (45min, 1423m).

> From here **Pic des Escaliers** (1472m) on the right can be climbed in five minutes. **Arthanolatzégagnia** (1530m) to the west is also easy (you can be there and back in 35 minutes). The prominent peak to the south is Pic d'Orhy (2017m), the most westerly 2000m peak in the Pyrenees. Looking

east-south-east you get your first good view of the High Pyrenees with the bare rock of Pic d'Anie and surrounding mountains.

Descend, initially left, but soon switch back and follow a well-engineered path which traverses the steep N slopes of Pic des Escaliers before descending its NE ridge to reach the road (1hr 15min). Turn right and follow the road to the E ridge, Crête Ugatzé. Turn left, NE, down a good track until the track switches back left at a col. Follow a path on the right-hand side of the ridge to reach another col (1hr 40min) and veer right past a shack. The waterpoint at the cattle trough is reliable. Follow the path to another col and follow a track on the right, which soon arrives at some cabins below yet another col (2hr).

You will need to follow waymarks very carefully for the next couple of hours as the route is not always obvious. Start by descending from the cabins then veer left to follow a succession of animal tracks as you traverse the S slopes of **Beloscare** (1173m) through rough open terrain and woodland. Eventually you reach a tarmac farm road at a col (2hr 50min, 1017m). Cross the road and take the track opposite which follows the ridge S and soon leads to the best campsites for some time. After crossing the

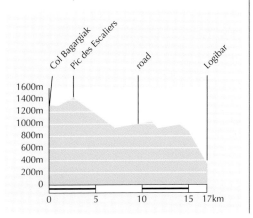

summit follow the grassy track down right, then veer left along the fence and fork left along a contouring path to cross the S ridge of Peak 1066 and descend the E ridge to reach a col (3hr 25min). At the far end of the col a path forks right to contour to the next col. Continue up the ridge before veering right of the next top. On returning to the ridge, follow the right-hand side of an old stone wall, veering left to pass a barn and passing an unreliable waterpoint as you contour back to the ridge. Pass to the right of more tops, fork right to follow the right-hand side of another wall down the ridge before following a small rough track which zigzags all the way down to a tarmac farm road (4hr 45min). Turn right and follow the road down, ignoring two right turns, to arrive at the **Auberge Logibar** (5hr, 375m) with a waterpoint.

FACILITIES FOR STAGE 8

Logibar

Auberge Logibar, gîte d'étape, chambres d'hôtes accommodation and bar-restaurant: tel 05 59 28 61 14, www.auberge-logibar.com

Hôtel-restaurant Etchémaïté: tel 05 59 28 61 45, www.hotel-etchemaite.fr

Chez Despouey, rooms, bar and small shop: tel 05 59 28 60 82, www.chambresdespouey.weebly.com

Larrau

Just over 2km W of Logibar, Larrau is a small town with accommodation, a campsite and small shop.

Camping Ixtila: tel 07 69 37 77 35, www.campingixtilalarrau.com

STAGE 9

Logibar to Sainte-Engrâce (Senta)

Start	Logibar
Distance	25km
Total ascent	1200m
Total descent	900m
Time	7hr 20min
High point	Col d'Anhaou (1383m)

This long stage starts with a climb up magnificent limestone gorges followed by easy walking along farm tracks and roads. Be aware that the polished limestone on this stage is very slippery when wet. In 2021 there was a deviation of the GR10 in place here while works took place on the first part of the route. That work is now completed and the normal route is open but keep an eye out for any deviation signs that nobody has remembered to remove!

Turn right along the road, cross the bridge and turn left up the road signed to Gorges d'Holzarté. Cross the Torrent

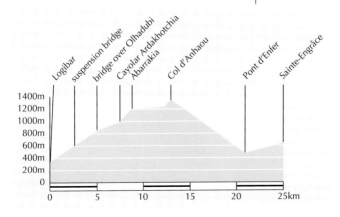

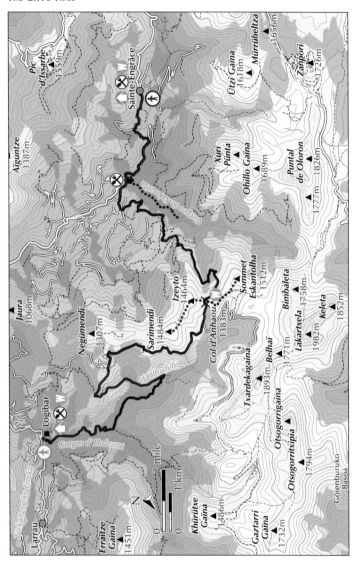

The suspension bridge over Gorges d'Olhadubi

d'Holzarté and follow the trail up the left-hand side of the **Gorges d'Holzarté** through thick beech forest. The path climbs high above the stream and reaches an impressive 70m-long swinging suspension bridge, 150m above the Ruisseau de Olhadubi (45min, 580m). ▶

Cross the bridge and continue to climb, eventually reaching a good track that provides the first campsites on the ascent. Turn left and climb gently to cross a stream a short time before reaching the main Olhadubi stream (840m, 1hr 50min) (camping possible). There are rock pools here in which you could cool off on a hot day. Cross the bridge, veer left and follow a path gradually climbing above the E slopes of the gorge. Shortly after passing two clear-looking streams you leave the woods. Continue climbing gently, then veer right onto the ridge (2hr 35min). ▶ Cheese may be available at Cayolar Ardakhotchia, 200m along the track on the right.

The GR10 goes right, straight up the ridge. Cross a track and keep climbing, passing just right of a tarmac farm road and veering left up to the farm buildings at Abarrakia

This bridge was first built by Italian engineers in 1920 in order to exploit the Holzarté forest.

The rare Egyptian vulture has been sighted here.

(3hr 20min, 980m). Turn right along the road, which soon becomes a dirt road, and contour roughly S passing several small farms before reaching the Cayolar d'Iguéloua and shortly afterwards a sharp right-hand bend (4hr 10min).

The GR10 leaves the track and climbs E up steep grass slopes on a faint path. Skirt the edge of a wood before climbing the final grass slopes to the **Col d'Anhaou** (4hr 35min, 1383m).

> Climbs from Col d'Anhaou include **Izeyto** (1464m) and **Sarimendi** (1484m) on the ridge to the left from here (up and down in 45 minutes) or **Sommet Eskantolha** (1512m) to the right (up and down in 35 minutes).

Follow the tarmac farm road down the other side of the col, soon passing a new cabin with waterpoint and reaching a farm, also with waterpoint. Go diagonally left down a grassy track, shortcutting a switchback in the road. Turn left on regaining the road, passing another waterpoint. ◄ Eventually, immediately after a switchback (5hr 15min), the GR10 veers left and descends steep grass slopes, crossing the road three times as it shortcuts the switchbacks. The path then veers left and follows an ancient path down to a stream. Cross and turn right along a grassy track, then fork right along a path to reach a complex junction. Fork right down the ancient path to arrive at the roadhead by a farm (5hr 55min). Keep straight on down the road until you turn down a path that goes off back right. Descend to join a track and cross a bridge over a narrow reservoir. Climb the concrete track on the other side to reach the D113 road (6hr 30min, 500m). Turn right, passing a road to the **Gorges de Kakouéta**.

As you descend you will see the tops of the vertical cliffs of the Gorges de Kakouéta to your right.

> The **Gorges de Kakouéta** are one of the most impressive natural features in this western part of the Pyrenees. There used to be an entrance fee which gave access to a slippery path up the gorge, passing a small waterfall to arrive at a massive cave. Although a very popular tourist attraction, the cliff

faces were never very stable and the use of safety helmets was compulsory. Sadly, though, it wasn't enough and in the summer of 2020 a young mother was killed by a rock fall. The gorges have remained firmly closed to the public ever since.

Continue up the road passing through Sainte-Engrâce (Bourg) and on to a road junction. ▶ The GR10 forks right to the church and Auberge Elichalt in **Sainte-Engrâce** (Senta) (7hr 20min, 630m).

The D113 forks left, passing a bar-restaurant after 800m and continuing to Arette-la Pierre-St-Martin.

FACILITIES FOR STAGE 9

Auberge Elichalt, gîte d'étape, chambres d'hôtes accommodation and bar-restaurant. Toilets and water are available to walkers and it should be possible to camp: tel 05 59 28 61 63, www.gites-burguburu.com

STAGE 10
Sainte-Engrâce (Senta) to Refuge Jeandel

Start	Sainte-Engrâce (Senta)
Distance	12km
Total ascent	1200m
Total descent	200m
Time	4hr 40min
High point	Col de la Pierre-St-Martin (1760m)

This final stage in the Basque Country sees the transition from rolling hills to the Alpine mountains. Stages 10 and 11 pass through complex limestone karst terrain and care is needed with navigation, especially in poor weather.

Continue down the road, forking right and then left along a track, right across a stream, then take the second left immediately afterwards. Follow this path, ignoring a

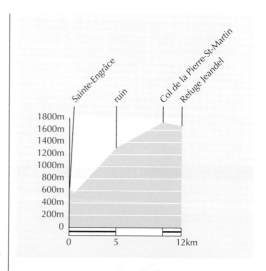

Le Gardien

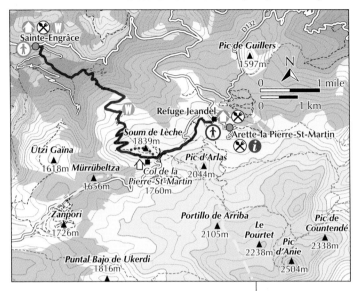

faint left fork before turning left at a clearer junction. You are soon heading along the bottom of the Ravin d'Arpedia. ▶ At a junction (45min) the GR10 goes sharp left, leaving the ravine and climbing steeply through the woods to reach a switchback in a grassy track (1hr 5min) where camping is possible. Turn right and right again up a path which crosses the track twice before turning right up the track. Soon after, turn left up a path to cross the track three more times before reaching a water trough with an unusual stone carving, Le Gardien (2hr 20min). Unfortunately there is no water!

Continue climbing and emerge from the wood into pasture (2hr 30min). Veer sharp right at a ruin and follow a path that is very faint in places with indistinct waymarks. Veer left round a ridge to reach a cattle trough with an unreliable waterpoint (2hr 50min). Head towards some small boulders where the path and waymarks become clearer and lead to another cattle trough with unreliable waterpoint. Turn sharp right and follow the

Notice the interesting flora at the bottom of this damp, sunless limestone gorge.

It would be easy to traverse Soum de Lèche (1839m) on the left from here or climb it from the Col de la Pierre-St-Martin (15min there and back).

waymarks, not the track. Take care as the animal tracks are more prominent than the GR10. Pick up a grassy track which veers sharp left at a corral and becomes a clear track as it zigzags to the top of the hill (4hr). ◄

The GR10 continues along the track to meet the D132 at the **Col de la Pierre-St-Martin** (4hr 10min, 1760m) on the border with Spain. Notice the entrance to an extremely deep cave by the junction. Borderstone 62, a basic bothy and picnic table are across the road.

Turn left along the road, then keep straight on along a track at the first switchback. Follow the track under two sets of ski lifts, ignore a track forking left and veer right to reach the N ridge of **Pic d'Arlas**. Turn right just before three concrete water tanks and follow the path down to **Refuge Jeandel** (4hr 40min, 1670m).

Refuge Jeandel has full refuge facilities and should be able to provide basic provisions. A 10-minute walk from there is the ski resort of Arette-la Pierre-St-Martin, which dominates the view to the E. The facilities are closed in May, June and September but you should be able to find a bar-restaurant and the tourist office open in July and August. There is a bus service to Oloron-Sainte-Marie connecting with the French rail system.

FACILITIES FOR STAGE 10

Tourist office, Arette-la Pierre-St-Martin: tel 05 59 66 20 09, www.lapierrestmartin.com

Refuge Jeandel (open all year), Arette-la Pierre-St-Martin: tel 05 59 66 14 46 or 06 20 07 19 89, www.refugejeandel.com

STAGE 11
Refuge Jeandel to Lescun

Start	Refuge Jeandel
Distance	15km
Total ascent	400m
Total descent	1200m
Time	5hr 25min
High point	Pas de l'Osque (1922m)

The GR10 now enters the High Pyrenees with all the problems and delights associated with high Alpine mountains as you walk through limestone karst scenery with towering limestone cliffs. Snow could be a problem in early season and the limestone will be very slippery in wet weather. It is very important to stay on the waymarked route as navigation errors made in karst terrain are very difficult to correct. Campsites are few and far between and your first water will be at the Cabane du Cap de la Baitch. At the end of the stage you could continue to Camping du Lauzart, with its gîte d'étape, which is 20 minutes into Stage 12. As is usual, the waymarking through the ski areas is poor.

Follow the track down from the refuge and veer sharp right at the bottom, then left and follow a good track heading SE. Ignore a right turn and follow the track past various buildings associated with the ski resort until, just after a short descent, the GR10 turns left along a faint path through a grassy area with good campsites (35min).

The **HRP** continues up the track before following an extremely complex route through magnificent limestone karst scenery over the Col d'Anie – from where you can scoot to the summit of the Pic d'Anie (2504m) for stellar views and the first real sensation of being in the high mountains – to rejoin the GR10 at the Cabane du Cap de la Baitch. In clear,

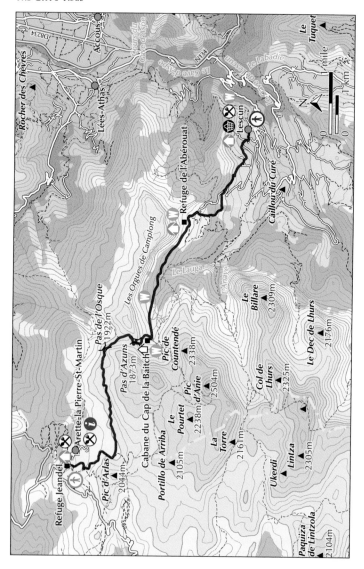

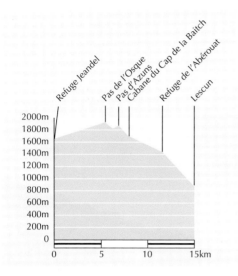

settled summer weather the route is simple enough
but the possibility of getting lost in the karstic maze
remains. In poor weather it's simply dangerous and
shouldn't be attempted by anyone without serious
high mountain experience.

Gradually veer left and climb through limestone
karst terrain. Cross a ski piste and eventually join a large
ski piste to reach the top of a chairlift in a scene of envi-
ronmental desecration (1hr 35min). It's easy to lose the
trail here. Veer left and descend to the bottom station of
the upper ski lift and look for the GR10 trail marker by
the first pylon on the ski lift.

You are now entering spectacular terrain. Climb
gently to a pass over a ridge, then traverse gently
down before climbing to a gap in the rock wall on
your right. After an easy scramble reach the **Pas de
l'Osque** (2hr 20min, 1922m). Traverse right, below the
cliffs, then veer up the valley on your right to arrive at
the **Pas d'Azuns** (2hr 45min, 1873m) where there is a

A distant view of the Pic du Midi d'Ossau from the descent to Lescun

There are excellent views down the valley towards the Pic du Midi d'Ossau, an icon of the French Pyrenees, and towards the dominating buttresses of Le Billare to the right.

magnificent view of Pic d'Anie (2504m). The path traverses left before starting an easy descent down grass slopes to the **Cabane du Cap de la Baitch** (3hr, 1689m) with a reliable waterpoint and a small room which may be available as a basic bothy. Good campsites. In summer the cabane is used by a shepherd and delicious brebis cheese is available to buy. ◄

Follow the path down, passing just below the Cabane d'Ardinet with waterpoint (3hr 15min). Enter the woods and follow the path which seems to go up as much as down and gets higher and higher above the valley floor. Ignore minor paths descending to the right. Eventually the path merges with a track shortly before reaching the **Refuge de l'Abérouat** (4hr 10min, 1442m).

This refuge is primarily intended for groups but it does take GR10 hikers with reservations, offering normal refuge facilities. If open, toilets and water will be available to hikers.

▶ Follow the road down a little then fork right down a grassy track and left at a stream with good campsites. Turn left down a path, fork right and turn right on regaining the road. Keep straight on down a track at the next bend in the road, fork second left, then left up a tarmac farm road. Turn right down a path, then left along a small tarmac road. Ignore a left turn, then, on a right-hand bend, turn left along a track, forking left after it has become a small tarmac road and follow it down to the war memorial at the centre of **Lescun** (5hr 25min, 900m).

In wet weather you may prefer to follow the road down to Lescun rather than the GR10, which can get very muddy.

A beautiful stone village, Lescun sits surrounded by fields in the middle of a vast cirque, which is perhaps better described as several cirques within one big cirque! If you want to pause for a few days then this is a great place to do so with numerous superb day hikes available around the village. As well as the tough hike to the summit of the Pic d'Anie there are the easy but superb walks to the Lac d'Ansabère or the Lac de Lhurs and the tougher route to Table des Trois Roi. Lescun has waterpoints, a small shop that stocks all types of camping gas, accommodation and bar-restaurants.

FACILITIES FOR STAGE 11

Refuge de l'Abérouat: tel 05 59 34 71 67, www.aberouat.fr

Lescun

Lescun is covered by the Vallée d'Aspe tourist office in Bedous: tel 05 59 34 57 57, www.tourisme-aspe.com

Gîte d'étape Maison de la Montagne offers a full meals service: tel 05 59 34 79 14

Hôtel du Pic d'Anie, chambres d'hôtes and gîte d'étape accommodation, offers breakfast and evening meals: tel 05 59 34 71 54, www.hebergement-picdanie.fr

Gîte les Estives, chambres d'hôtes: tel 05 59 34 77 60, www.estives-lescun.com

See also Stage 12 for facilities available heading out of Lescun.

STAGE 12
Lescun to Etsaut

Start	Lescun
Distance	16km
Total ascent	800m
Total descent	1100m
Time	5hr 25min
High point	Col de Barrancq (1601m)

This is an easy day following roads and tracks through farmland before the crossing of the wooded Col de Barrancq.

Continue steeply downhill out of the village, then turn sharp left and right and descend to cross **Le Gave de Lescun** on the Pont du Moulin. Keep straight on up a steep stony path that climbs to **Camping du Lauzart**, which has a gîte d'étape (20min).

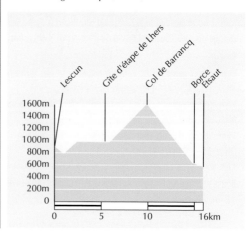

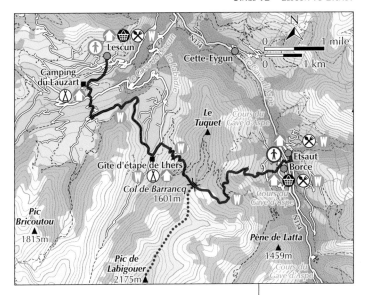

Turn right along the road, keeping straight on at
crossroads and then turning sharp left up a track. Fork
right up a path then go straight across a road and up a
cobbled lane. Turn right at the next road and then sharp
left up a woodland path (50min). Turn left along a road,
then fork left down a path before a gate in the road and
then fork right and pass between houses where there is
a waterpoint. Continue down the path, cross a stream
and you are soon contouring through steep woods. Veer
right through a gate to leave the woods, fork left along a
track and contour. Veer right onto a farm road and cross
the river where there is a picnic table. Continue to a
T-junction (1hr 45min, 997m) on the Plateau de Lhers.

> Gîte d'étape de Lhers is about 150m to the right.
> The gîte d'étape offers meals and drinks service.
> Camping is possible. There are toilets and a water-
> point in the aire de camping-car.

A Dutch hiker on the Pic de Labigouer ridge

The GR10 goes left, then forks right up a wide track before turning right up a faint path and climbing steeply up the grassy hillside. Veer right and start to zigzag up the slope, which is exceptional for its wild flowers. Turn right when you reach a track and follow it as it zigzags through the wood. There is a waterpoint (running well summer 2022) and campsites at the second switchback (2hr 35min). Go straight on at a junction. This smaller track soon becomes a path as it zigzags up the hill. There follows a staggered crossing of a grass track before you rejoin the main forest track. Immediately after the first left-hand switchback take a path forking right, then up a small track and left off it to reach the wooded **Col de Barrancq** (3hr 35min, 1601m).

The path on the right could be followed to **Pic de Labigouer** (2175m) (there and back in 160min). This easy ascent gives magnificent views back to the Pic d'Anie range, forward to the Pic du Midi d'Ossau and north to the spectacular peaks of the border ridge through which the HRP passes.

The GR10 descends steeply down a path and into open pasture where camping should be possible. You cross several small clear-looking streams and pass through a short section of wood before leaving the pasture just left of the Cabane d'Udapet, which has a waterpoint (4hr, 1401m). Follow the track down, forking right along a path after crossing a stream, then right and left to descend steeply before crossing a stream and descending more gently onto open hillside. Descend and eventually switch back right to recross the stream. Continue descending, ignoring a path across a bridge signed to Chambres d'hôtes l'Espiatet, to reach a tarmac farm road (4hr 55min). Turn left and almost immediately left again, then sharp right. Turn left down an old cobbled path (slippery when wet) along the fences of the Parc d'Ours.

> This **wildlife park** rescues abandoned, unwanted, injured or ill animals to allow them to recuperate. There is a range of Pyrenean fauna in the park but it is best known for its brown bears: www. parc-ours.fr.

Continue descending to reach roads on the edge of **Borce** and down to the church (5hr 15min, 660m). The bar-restaurant with a gîte d'étape and a small shop is to the right. The GR10 goes left, passing several waterpoints and public toilets. Just before the edge of the village, turn sharp right alongside the stream. Cross the main road on a footbridge and then the bridge across the river to arrive at the S end of **Etsaut** (5hr 25min, 597m).

> Turn left for La Randonneur bar-restaurant, which is run by a real character and offers just the sort of filling meals you want after a day hiking. Also close to the church are gîtes d'étape, picnic site and unreliable waterpoint. The Maison du Parc, with interesting displays and an information desk, is at the N end of the small village. The branch railway line from Pau to Oloron-Ste-Marie has been

extended to Bedous and there is a bus service from Bedous to Col du Somport (via Canfranc Estación in Spain), which passes through Etsaut.

FACILITIES FOR STAGE 12

Lescun

Camping du Lauzart, with gîte d'étape: tel 05 59 34 51 77, www.camping-gite-lescun-pyrenees.com

Gîte d'étape de Lhers, English spoken: tel 05 59 34 75 39 or 06 70 20 45 86, www.gite-camping-lhers.com

Borce

Gîte le Communal: tel 05 59 34 86 40, www.lecommunal.fr

Chambre d'hôtes l'Espiatet: tel 07 50 35 89 13, www.lespiatet.com

Chambre d'hôtes Maison Bergoun: tel 06 42 69 47 45, www.bergoun.com

Etsaut

Etsaut and Borce are covered by the Vallée d'Aspe tourist office in Bedous: tel 05 59 34 57 57, www.tourisme-aspe.com

La Randonneur, bar-restaurant, 05 59 34 16 13

Gîte d'étape la Garbure, full meals service, behind the church: tel 05 59 34 88 98, www.garbure.net

2 ETSAUT TO BAGNÈRES-DE-LUCHON

KEY INFORMATION

Distance	253km
Total ascent	14,400m
Time	86hr walking
Maps	IGN Carte de Randonnées 1:50,000 maps 3–5

This is the most spectacular section of the GR10. The route will take you right across the central Pyrenees and see you labouring up high passes which are likely to be snow-dappled well into summer and descending into densely forested valleys. The real scenic highlights are found in the areas around the Pic du Midi d'Ossau, Vignemale, Gavarnie and the lake-splattered Néouvielle massif.

Pic du Midi d'Ossau from Lac Gentau (Stage 13)

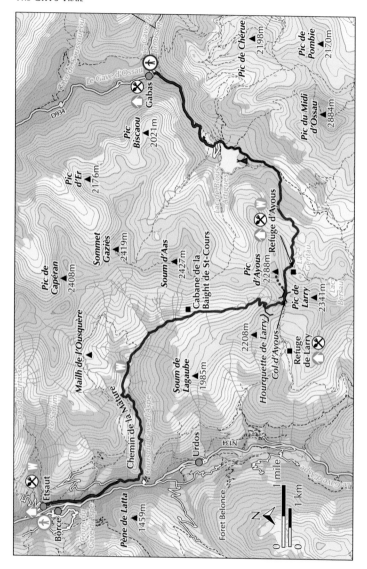

STAGE 13
Etsaut to Gabas

Start	Etsaut
Distance	25km
Total ascent	1600m
Total descent	1200m
Time	7hr 50min
High point	Col d'Ayous (2185m)

The GR10 follows the spectacular Chemin de la Mâture, a rising traverse cut into a near vertical rockface. Although it can look a little daunting the path is safe (this author has walked it several times with his children) in summer weather conditions. However, if there was ice or snow on the path then it would be very dangerous indeed. The next challenge is crossing the Col d'Ayous (snow could be a problem in early season) from which there are spectacular views of the Pic du Midi d'Ossau. Camping opportunities are very limited until you reach the bothy about three hours into the stage. This is a long stage and many people sensibly prefer to break it up by staying at the wonderfully located Refuge d'Ayous and then having a short day walking down to Gabas to prepare for the arduous Stage 14.

From Etsaut head S along the old main road up the E side of the river to the Pont de Cebers, where there is a car park and some interesting information boards. Keep straight on along the left-hand bank to reach a switchback in the road where you veer right to start the **Chemin de la Mâture** (35min). ▶

Notice how the Fort du Portalet, visible on your right, dominates the ravine of the Gave d'Aspé.

The **Chemin de la Mâture** was cut into near-vertical limestone cliffs in the time of Louis XIV in the 17th century to transport timber through the Sescoué ravine. The massive construction task required 3000 *radeleurs* (navvies). Timber would have been taken down the trail on specially

Chemin de la Mâture

designed ox carts and then formed into rafts and floated all the way down to Bayonne. This monumental task was to provide the timber needed to modernise the French Navy, illustrating not only the importance of the navy but the vast economic drain it must have been on the country.

The trail is now just a narrow cut in a near-vertical cliff face. It ascends gently upward along the gorge. Fork right at the top of the gorge, near the cabins of Grange Perry, which are in a clearing on the left (1hr 50min, 1210m). There's a reliable water source here and camping is possible. The cabin is used by shepherds in summer. Contour through the woods before forking left at a junction (2hr 5min) and climbing. Turn right at the next junction and then cross a stream. The path now passes through a mixture of rough open terrain and woodland. Fork right and pass a spring-fed pipe immediately before crossing a stream on a bridge. After another right fork you eventually cross a main stream and continue up the left-hand side of the valley, entering the national park (bivouac regulations apply) just before reaching the **Cabane de la Baight de St-Cours** (3hr 30min, 1560m) at the bottom of the upper pasture. This bothy is reserved for herdsmen from mid June to late September.

Cross the stream on a small bridge (3hr 50min) and continue up the right-hand side of the stream. The path is faint in places and you might lose it, but it takes you into the upper corrie, which is likely to have the last water on the ascent. Switch back right from the corrie and climb most of the way to the **Hourquette de Larry**. Just before reaching the col, the now-clear path veers left and continues to climb to a little col (5hr 15min, 2125m) from where a path descends right to the Refuge de Larry. The GR10 ignores this and continues roughly E to the **Col d'Ayous** (5hr 25min, 2185m). ▶ There are magnificent views from here, and throughout the descent, to the Pic du Midi d'Ossau to the E, probably the most photographed mountain in the Pyrenees. The GR10 descends

Pic d'Ayous (2288m) on the left is an easy climb from here (up and down in 25min).

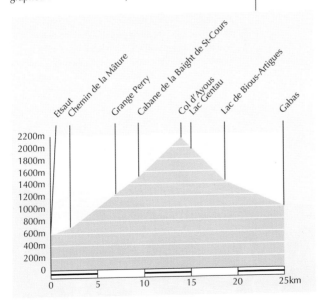

101

left on a multi-stranded path to arrive at a junction by **Lac Gentau** (6hr 15min, 1960m).

If you turn right you will reach Refuge d'Ayous, on the W shore of the lake, in about 7min. This is a popular refuge with full refuge facilities and a waterpoint. The NW shore of the lake is excellent for swimming once the water has warmed up. Camping is normally allowed next to the lake but it has been banned in the past. If planning to camp, check with refuge staff in advance. Whether you camp or stay at the refuge it's one of the most gorgeous potential overnight stops on the trail and a stay here is a good way to break up the otherwise long hike. If you choose to spend the night at the Refuge d'Ayous it is strongly recommended to add in a simply gorgeous loop around a series of lakes to the south of the refuge. Leaving the refuge turn right (south) and zig-zag uphill to a plateau-like area dotted with several lakes including, at the end of the line, the Lac Bersau (2083m). Heading around the eastern side of the lake cross a small ridge overlooking the thumb-shaped Pic Castérau (2227m) and then descend hard downhill to your left (don't follow the more obvious trail straight ahead – it leads into Spain) to arrive at the Lac Castérou. Continue straight ahead, losing altitude

Pic du Midi d'Ossau from Lac d'Ayous

all the time, until you reach a trail junction by some summer shepherd huts and a cement road (authorised vehicles only). Take the left trail and head northwest across a vast flat pasture until you reach the edge of the beech forest and meet up with the GR10 leading down to the Lac de Bious Artigues. This loop back to where you re-meet the GR10 takes about 2hr.

Continue down the well-trod GR10 passing to the left of two more lakes, then veer left and descend through pasture and then woodland to reach the track along the Gave de Bious (6hr 35min, 1540m). Turn left and descend beside the stream and cross to the right-hand bank before passing a sign to an aire de bivouac on the left as you approach the **Lac de Bious-Artigues**. Swimming is possible from the bivouac area. As you follow the E shore of the reservoir you pass a pony trekking centre with a snack bar and a canoe hire centre before reaching a large car park, with toilets, at the roadhead at the E tip of the reservoir (7hr, 1430m).

The GR10 descends down the D231 road, short-cutting the second switchback on the right, before following the road down. As you approach Gabas fork left down a path. Reach the D934, the main road (7hr 45min, 1035m). **Gabas**, with two hotels and a bar-restaurant but no shop, is just down the road to the left (7hr 50min). ▸

If you don't need Gabas you can follow the GR10 right up the grassy track.

FACILITIES FOR STAGE 13

Refuge d'Ayous (open year round, staffed mid May June to early October): tel 05 59 05 37 00, www.refuge-ayous.fr

Gabas

The tourist office in Laruns, about 6km to the N, covers this area:
tel 05 59 05 31 41, www.ossau-pyrenees.com

Chambres d'Hôtes l'Estibère: tel 06 88 38 19 75,
https://chambres-dhotes-lestibere.business.site

Hôtel-restaurant le Biscaü: tel 05 59 05 31 37, www.hotel-vallee-ossau-biscau.fr

STAGE 14
Gabas to Gourette

Start	Gabas
Distance	23km
Total ascent	1500m
Total descent	1200m
Time	8hr 55min
High point	Hourquette d'Arre (2465m)
Warning	The section along the Corniche des Alhas is not for those who suffer from vertigo or those with young children in tow.

An early start is recommended for one of the longest and toughest stages on the GR10. Lower down, there is a section of exposed ledges cut from vertical cliffs with an alternative route for those of a nervous disposition. There follows a magnificent crossing of the Hourquette d'Arre. This col can hold snow deep into June and is likely to be dangerous in the morning when the snow is icy but should not present a serious problem once the snow has softened. Care will be needed with navigation, even in good visibility, and it will be difficult in mist, especially if snow is covering the waymarks.

Head back up the road to the junction with the GR10 and fork right along a grassy track which cuts back to the road. Go straight across and follow the 'old' road which merges with the **D934**. Follow the road, then turn left along a path just below the dam at Artouste (20min, 1130m). Cross the stream and veer left, roughly E, rising gently and switch back N before starting to descend and crossing a small stream (55min). Join a forestry track and follow the 'main' track to a signpost marking a split in the GR10 (1hr 15min, 1112m).

Alternative route to avoid Corniche des Alhas
The Pont du Goua variation, intended for those of a nervous disposition, follows the forest track down to the Pont

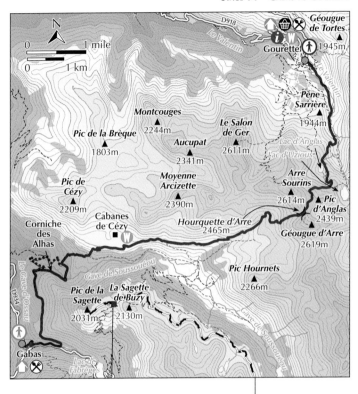

The Corniche des Alhas is narrower than the Chemin de la Mâture in Stage 13 and there is a greater feeling of exposure, but there is a hand-line along its length. It would be interesting to see what would happen if two large groups travelling in opposite directions met. Having said all of that, most people, even those with vertigo, would have no problems with the route.

Corniche des Alhas

du Goua and then climbs up a track to rejoin the main variation described below. It will take a little longer, but avoids the exposed section of the Corniche des Alhas.

Fork right up a path to approach the **Corniche des Alhas**, which is a ledge cut out of the rock on near-vertical limestone cliffs.

After completing the Corniche des Alhas you arrive at a bridge over the cascades of the **Gave de Soussouéou**. Care is needed if you want to access the water. Cross and continue to a junction with a small track (1hr 45min, 1125m). ◄

The Pont du Goua route rejoins here from the left.

Turn right and start climbing steeply up the old miners' path, keeping straight on at a junction at Houn de Mouscabarous (2hr 35min, 1361m). The steep climb eventually ends at the foot of some limestone cliffs with overhangs, which could provide shelter in a storm (3hr).

A few more switchbacks see you at the top of the cliffs after which there is a gently rising traverse to the E below the crags on the slopes of the Pic de Cézy (1948m). You briefly turn NW into the valley (3hr 25min). Just off route, 7min up the valley, is Cabanes de Cézy with good camp-sites and a waterpoint just below the main cabin. ▶

The GR10 only enters the mouth of the valley before turning back E and continuing below the crags of la Petite Arcizette (2293m). Water trickling from a spring above (3hr 45min) may provide your first on route water for a very long time.

> The **Alpine chough** is fairly common in the Pyrenees, and in this valley the yellow-billed Alpine chough and the red-billed chough have been sighted together. Choughs are easily identified as they are the only all-black birds with coloured bills.

A waymarked variation of the GR10 goes up this valley, over Col de Lurdé (1948m) to Eaux-Bonnes, then you can follow the GRP Tour de la Vallée d'Ossau to Gourette.

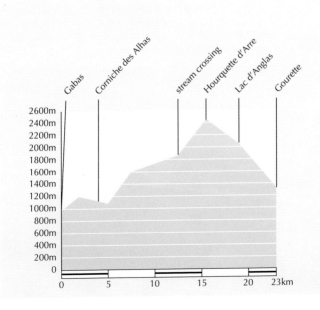

Across the valley you will see and hear **le Petit Train d'Artouste**, which claims to be the highest train in Europe. A gondola takes tourists from the Lac de Fabréges up the Pic de la Sagette to the terminus of the railway, which traverses the north slopes of the Crête de la Sagette to reach Lac d'Artouste (1997m).

Cross a trickling stream and climb more steeply to cross the main stream in the valley, possibly getting wet feet, or even perhaps on an ice bridge (4hr 40min). Follow the path, which climbs to the right of the stream. This path may be under snow well into summer. Cross a major side stream (5hr) and the main stream and continue climbing until just below some ancient iron mines (5hr 25min, 2099m). This is the last opportunity to camp near water on the ascent.

Turn right, S, across a bowl, which could hold snow into the start of July, and then veer left, E, and climb the switchbacks. The final ascent will either be up snowfield or a path through the scree to reach the **Hourquette d'Arre** (6hr 40min, 2465m).

The approach to Hourquette d'Arre

If there is still snow on this west-facing slope it is likely to be very icy in the morning and is steep enough to be very dangerous. You should not attempt to climb it unless you have crampons or unless it is possible to kick good steps in the snow. It may be more feasible in the afternoon when the snow has softened. Unusually, the descent route is likely to be much safer in snow than the ascent route.

▶ You are not descending to the obvious Lac d'Uzious straight ahead to the E but to a lake hidden away to the NNE. The GR10 climbs slightly to the N before roughly contouring NNE across a plateau, which will hold snow well into summer. Pass left of a small bothy to reach the col W of Pic d'Anglas. Start the descent, initially NW before gradually veering to the E. A complex route has been carefully waymarked to avoid most of the snowfields. Eventually the route forks left and works its way down through the crags to the SE of **Lac d'Anglas** and through the mine workings to the NE corner of the lake (7hr 40min, 2068m). The large snowfields feeding the lake mean it will not be comfortable for swimming in early summer.

A path is marked on some maps up Géougue d'Arre (2619m) to the right. It does exist but from below it looks more of a mountaineers' route than a walkers' route.

Cross the outlet stream and descend steeply, turning right at a junction. Fork right on meeting a grassy track, ignore a right turn then fork right down a path. Go straight across a track (8hr 30min) and into the woods. Cross a bridge over a cascade, turning right and left at the tennis courts to arrive at a car park at the top of Gourette (8hr 50min). ▶ It is a few minutes down the road to the tourist office in the Maison de Gourette at the centre of **Gourette** (8hr 55min, 1346m) where there is a waterpoint.

In the unlikely event of your not wanting any of the facilities of Gourette you can start Stage 15 by taking the small road climbing E from the car park.

Gourette is a ski resort but most of the facilities will be closed in summer or only be open in July and August when the supermarket should be open. Intersport stocks Coleman-style camping gas. There is a bus service from Gourette to Pau via Laruns.

FACILITIES FOR STAGE 14

Gourette

Tourist office: tel 05 59 05 12 17, www.gourette.com

Refuge CAF de Gourette, hidden away by the car park at the NE end of the resort, has full refuge facilities (open June to mid September): tel 05 59 05 10 56, https://chaletdegourette.ffcam.fr

Hôtel-restaurant la Boule de Neige (open mid June to mid September): tel 05 59 05 10 05, www.hotel-bouledeneige.com

Hôtel le Glacier: tel 05 59 05 10 18, www.hotel-leglacier-gourette.com

Hôtel l'Amoulat (open mid June to early September): tel 05 59 05 12 06; www.hotel-amoulat.com

STAGE 15

Gourette to Arrens-Marsous

Start	Gourette
Distance	15km
Total ascent	900m
Total descent	1300m
Time	5hr 10min
High point	Col de Tortes (1799m), Col de Saucède (1525m)

This is a short, easy stage crossing two low passes. Care must be used in navigation as the paths are not always well defined.

Return to the car park at the top of Gourette and follow a small tarmac road that climbs from the far left corner. This soon becomes a track and zigzags up the hill. Just after the track has levelled off, fork right up a path, switch back up through the forest and then climb

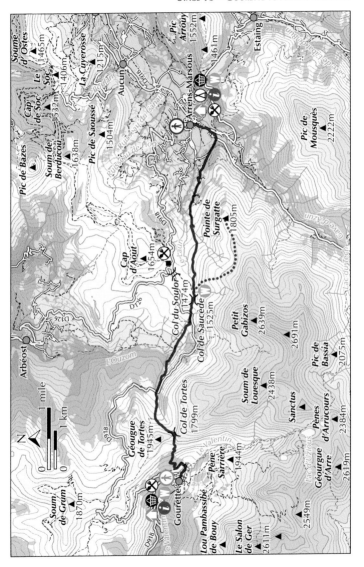

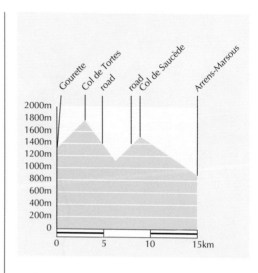

steeply as the path weaves a route through crags and fallen boulders to arrive at the **Col de Tortes** (1hr 25min, 1799m).

The path descends through pasture on the left-hand side of the valley to reach the **D918** (2hr). Camping is possible beside a stream towards the bottom of the descent. The GR10 used to follow the road, but it is rather dangerous and you now go straight across the road and descend steeply. After crossing the stream the path descends high above it before reaching the bottom (2hr 35min, 1131m), at the head of L'Ouzom valley, where there will probably be a snow cave in the avalanche debris well into summer. ◄

A trail veers off left here, the GRP Tour du Val d Azun, which meanders in a lovely loop around pond-dotted pastures.

Climb the pasture to the right of the barn, cross the stream and continue climbing to reach a track shortly before the D918 road (3hr 20min). Turn left along the road, then right through pasture to reach the **Col de Saucède** (3hr 45min, 1525m), and the waterpoint there. Take the track ENE for a short short distance before forking right down a path. If you continue down this track you could reach the bar-restaurants on the Col du Soulor

A snow cave in avalanche debris, l'Ouzom valley

in about 10min. Immediately before a small stone barn, a faint path goes right signed to Pointe de Surgatte (1805m). ▶

Cross the stream immediately after passing the barn and climb a little before starting a gradual descent high above the stream. Keep a close eye on the waymarks as the path is often less distinct than the many animal tracks on the hillside. Follow a small ridge for a bit then drop down to a stream on the right. Follow it down, cross and continue down to a cottage (4hr 25min). Follow the track down through farmland, ignoring side turns, before merging with a tarmac farm road (4hr 40min). Keep straight on down a track when the road becomes a switchback, then turn left along a road and back right down a path to reach the old bridge, Pont de Lapadé, across the Gave d'Arrens (5hr). ▶

Turn left for the tourist office in the centre of **Arrens-Marsous** (5hr 10min, 878m), which has public toilets and some interesting displays.

It is an easy climb to this peak, which is not a major mountain but the start of a knife-edge ridge dropping steeply down towards Arrens-Marsous (up and down in 90min).

If you don't require the facilities in Arrens-Marsous you could cross the bridge and start Stage 16.

Arrens-Marsous is a village with a number of small shops, bar-restaurants and limited accommodation. There is a waterpoint near the church. There are two campsites and the Proxi Supermarket, which sells original and easy-clic camping gas, about 700m along the road heading NE out of the village. There is a bus service to Lourdes.

FACILITIES FOR STAGE 15

Arrens-Marsous

The tourist office is in the Maison Val d'Azun: tel 05 62 97 49 49, www.valdazun.com

Gîte-auberge Camelat, gîte d'étape, chambres d'hôtes accommodation and meals: tel 06 07 94 23 93

Centre Vacances de La Salamandre has a gîte d'étape: tel 0800 65 65 00, https://centrevacances-lasalamandre.com

Camping La Hèche: tel 05 62 97 02 64, www.campinglaheche.com

Camping Mialanne: tel 05 62 92 67 14, https://campingmialanne.fr

STAGE 16
Arrens-Marsous to Refuge d'Ilhéou

Start	Arrens-Marsous
Distance	20km
Total ascent	1600m
Total descent	500m
Time	6hr 50min; alternative route 7hr 30min
High point	Col d'Ilhéou (2242m)

In good weather it is suggested that you follow the Tour du Val d'Azun, rather than the GR10, from Arrens-Marsous to Estaing. This route is more direct and more scenic than the GR10, but does involve more ascent and is slightly longer. The main feature of the stage is the long climb of the Col d'Ilhéou from the Lac d'Estaing. In previous editions of this guide the stage continued all the way to Cauterets but that will be too far for the average hiker. An alternative way to break the long section from Arrens-Marsous to Cauterets would be to stay at the Gîte d'étape les Viellettes or other accommodation in the Estaing area.

Return to the Pont de Lapadé, cross the bridge and turn left and follow the middle of three tracks to a junction with a signpost.

Alternative route on the Tour du Val d'Azun
Turn sharp right at the signpost up a good path with red/yellow waymarks, which zigzags through the Arboretum Arrens-Marsous to a road. Cross and follow a path which continues zigzagging, approaching a stream before reaching the N ridge of Pic de Habouret. Veer right along the ridge to a small col (1hr 5min) and descend alongside the wall. Four minutes later fork right on a gently rising traverse, cross a fence on a ridge and continue, passing a spring, to reach a small col on the NE ridge of Pic de Mousquès (1hr 40min).

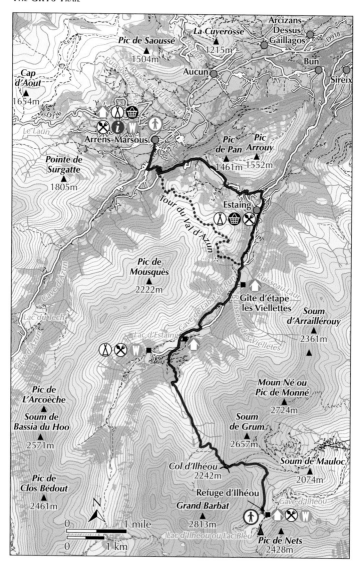

Pont de Lapadé over Gave d'Azun, Arrens-Marsous

Descend right to a better-defined col on the E ridge, cross a fence and descend left before zigzagging down to an old barn at the top of the woods. Pass right of the barn, cross a stream and veer left, descending to cross another stream. Eventually recross the stream before reaching the D103 at the Pont de Miaous, S of Estaing (2hr 30min) where you rejoin the GR10.

The GR10 continues roughly E, ignoring paths off to the left and right, to cross a stream where you switch back right and fork left to reach the road (35min). Turn left and soon take a shortcut left on a long right-hand bend. Turn left on regaining the road to reach the Col des Bordères (1hr, 1156m). The GR10 follows a path which goes up left just after the drive to a bar-restaurant. Turn left on returning

117

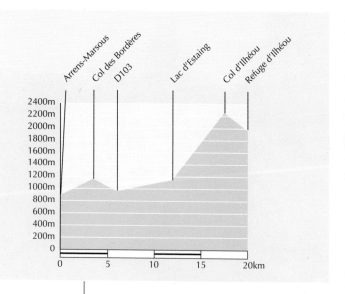

to the road. Take the shortcut on the right, after which you continue down the road to the next shortcut, veering right at a sharp left-hand bend. Go straight across the road when you next meet it and then turn left along another road. Pass between the church and the cemetery and then turn right to reach the D103 road on the floor of the valley (1hr 35min).

> If you want Camping Pyrénées Natura you should turn right along the road. The four-star campground has special rates for hikers as well as a small shop and snack bar.

The GR10 goes straight across the road and river and follows roads, tracks and paths on the E side of the river before rejoining the D103 at a bridge (1hr 35min). Cross the bridge and then turn left along a path along the right-hand bank of the **Gave de Labat**, eventually recrossing the river and returning to the D103. Turn right along the road (1hr 50min). ▸

Pass a turning on the left to the **Gîte d'étape les Viellettes**, which is about 200m back from the road, and continue to Camping la Pose, a basic campground (2hr 10min). The GR10 goes right from here and follows a small path along the hillside before returning to the road at Louyous farm (2hr 35min). There is another 'shortcut' along a grassy path just left of the road before you reach the Hôtel-restaurant du Lac d'Estaing (2hr 45min). Follow the road along the left-hand shore of the **Lac d'Estaing** (the far side of the lake is best for swimming) and fork left up a path on a right-hand bend (2hr 55min, 1161m).

The alternative route soon rejoins from the right.

> If you continue about 500m along the road to the end of the lake you will find a bar-restaurant, campground, toilets, water, picnic tables and a pony trekking centre.

Follow the waymarks carefully as the GR10 crosses many tracks as it climbs steeply through the conifer plantation forest (the rest of the forest in this valley is a natural deciduous forest and is a visual treat in October) and passes the Cabane d'Arriousec (3hr 35min, 1400m) as you approach the top of the forest. Continue up the track into the open, cutting short switchbacks on the right, then straight across the track. Follow the path up the left-hand side of the valley, high above the stream. You will probably cross several small side streams before eventually crossing the main stream (4hr 35min) on a bridge, if it hasn't been washed away! This will probably be your last water on the climb.

Climb to a cattle pen (5hr). The Cabanes de Barbat are on your right but the GR10 climbs left. Be careful to follow the waymarks on both ascent and descent of the col ahead as the 'path' is not always clear and there are many animal tracks to confuse. The path veers right and climbs easily, but steeply, to the grassy **Col d'Ilhéou** (6hr 5min, 2242m) where there are excellent but exposed campsites.

From the Cabanes de Barbat you could make a short deviation SE to the little jade-coloured Lac du Barbat wedged below the intimidating Grand Bardat (2813m). Despite only being a 30min return detour very few GR10 hikers are even aware of the existence of this lake.

Descend easily down the grassy valley. ◄ The GR10 continues down past the Cabanes d'Arras to a path junction beside a stream (6hr 25min). Turn right, cross two streams and continue to the right of a small knoll, then traverse roughly S before the final descent to the **Lac d'Ilhéou** and the **Refuge d'Ilhéou**, with full refuge facilities, at the NE tip of the lake (6hr 50min, 1988m). Swimming is easiest from the rocks by the 'aire de bivouac', which is about 8min along the S shore of the lake.

After 5min a path forks left to the Crête du Lys from where ski lifts, operating in July and August, could take you all the way down to Cauterets.

FACILITIES FOR STAGE 16

Between Estaing and Lac d'Estaing

Camping Pyrénées Natura: tel 05 26 97 45 44, www.camping-pyrenees-natura.com

Gîte d'étape les Viellettes, accommodation and meals: tel 06 43 87 14 24, www.auberge-lac-estaing.com

Camping la Pose: tel 06 82 17 22 53

Lac d'Estaing

Camping Lac d'Estaing: tel 05 62 97 24 46

Lac d'Ilhéou

Refuge d'Ilhéou (open year round, staffed June to early October): tel 05 62 92 07 18 or 06 79 08 20 64, www.refuge-ilheou.csvss.fr

STAGE 17

Refuge d'Ilhéou to Cauterets

Start	Refuge d'Ilhéou
Distance	8km
Total ascent	0m
Total descent	1100m
Time	2hr 15min
High point	Refuge d'Ilhéou (1988m)

This downhill stage is not much more than a rest day and you could continue to Pont d'Espagne as described in Stage 18. If you don't need Cauterets you could stray off the GR10 and follow a direct, and magnificent, route to Pont d'Espagne over Col de la Haugade as described in Stage 17A.

Follow the track from the refuge for about 100m to a junction. The GR10 continues left down the track, taking a shortcut right. ▶ Turn right on rejoining the track. The next shortcut is on the left, then straight across on the next meeting of the track. Rejoin the track for a short distance then stay right of the stream (55min, 1481m) when

The right turn here is for the 'aire de bivouac' and the alternative route to the Pont d'Espagne via the Col de la Haugade.

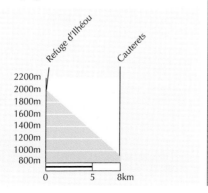

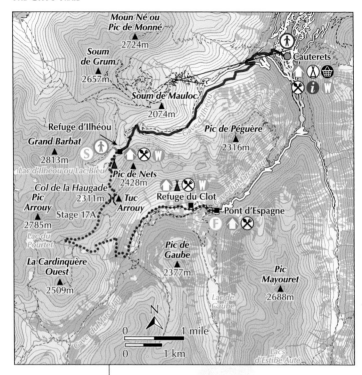

the track crosses the **Gave d'Ilhéou** to arrive at the car park at the base of the ski slopes.

Descend, forking left to stay beside the stream, and then roughly contour before descending alongside a wall and along a walled path to reach a road by a farm (1hr 40min). Turn left, then fork right down a track into the woods. Turn sharp right under the ski lift, then sharp left down a path and zigzag down to regain the road. Descend right then keep straight on down a path at the next sharp bend. Turn left at a junction and then descend a flood defence wall into **Cauterets**. Turn right and left to reach the tourist office, with public toilets, in the town centre (2hr 15min, 913m).

Gave d'Ilhéou

Pretty Cauterets has all the facilities you would expect from a major mountain resort. The attraction would have originally been based on the spas associated with the thermal springs but it is now skiing and walking which attract people. The Carrefour supermarket is down Avenue Leclerc, to the left. Just beyond the tourist office turn left down the narrow Rue Richelieu for a waterpoint, Hôtels Christian and Lion d'Or and the Catena ironmongers, which stocks all types of camping gas. Gîte d'étape de le Pas de l'Ours is along Rue de la Raillère, south from the tourist office. Gîte d'étape Beau Soleil is in Rue Maréchal Joffre, south from Thermes de César. Gîte d'étape le Cluquet, 300m north of the ski lift on the Avenue du Docteur Domer, provides the most basic and cheapest accommodation and also accepts small tents. There are seven campgrounds to the north of town. The tourist office suggests la Prairie might cater best for backpackers. There are bus connections to Lourdes, Luz-Saint-Sauveur and Gavarnie and a shuttle bus service to Pont d'Espagne. If you want a few days break from the GR10 there are many excellent walks in the mountains all around Cauterets.

FACILITIES FOR STAGE 17

Tourist office in Cauterets: tel 05 62 92 50 50, www.cauterets.com

Only a small selection of the accommodation in Cauterets is listed here.

Gîte d'étape Beau Soleil: tel 05 62 92 53 52 or 06 84 22 49 37, www.gite-beau-soleil.fr

Gîte d'étape le Pas de l'Ours: tel 05 62 92 58 07 or 06 14 01 46 92, www.lepasdelours.com

Gîte d'étape le Cluquet: tel 05 62 92 52 95 or 06 74 81 66 22, www.gite-lecluquet-cauterets.com

Hôtel Christian: tel 05 62 92 50 04, www.hotel-christian.fr

Hôtel le Lion d'Or: tel 05 62 92 52 87, www.liondor.eu

Camping la Prairie: tel 07 86 49 19 78, www.laprairiecamping.com

STAGE 17A

Refuge d'Ilhéou to the Pont d'Espagne
(via Col de la Haugade)

Start	Refuge d'Ilhéou
Distance	10km
Total ascent	400m
Total descent	900m
Time	4hr 10min
High point	Col de la Haugade (2378m)

Assuming you are intending to follow the main variation via the Hourquette d'Ossoue (see Stage 18) and you don't need the facilities at Cauterets, you could follow the magnificent high-level shortcut from the Refuge d'Ilhéou to the Pont d'Espagne via the Col de la Haugade (2378m). This route is rougher and less well waymarked than the GR10 and is only recommended for the experienced walker in good weather and only when the route is clear of snow. The route has occasional waymarks and lots of cairns on the critical descent route. There is no water on the ascent or until well down the descent.

▶ Follow the track from the refuge for about 100m to a junction. Turn right along the SW shore of the Lac d'Ilhéou to reach an aire de bivouac. Follow a good mountain path left from here and switchback up rough terrain to reach a corrie. Climb the left-hand side of the corrie to reach a grassy col, which provides excellent exposed, dry campsites (1hr 10min, 2311m). This is not the top of the climb! Fork right and climb to the **Col de la Haugade** (1hr 25min, 2378m).

From here a faint path goes down gently, diagonally right, roughly SSW, crossing boulderfields. ▶ The path eventually emerges at the outlet stream of the upper of the Lacs de l'Embarrat (2hr 10min). Turn sharp left and

For route map, see Stage 17.

Don't be tempted by a more direct steep descent shown on some maps.

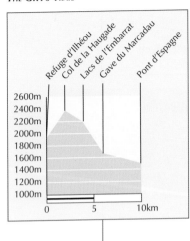

Refuge d'Ilhéou
Col de la Haugade
Lacs de l'Embarrat
Gave du Marcadau
Pont d'Espagne

2600m
2400m
2200m
2000m
1800m
1600m
1400m
1200m
1000m

0   5   10km

follow the main path past the lower lake and then away from the stream, descending through woods before veering right again as it zigzags down to a bridge across **Gave du Marcadau** (3hr 20min). Follow the path down the left-hand side of the valley, passing a small rough bothy after 10min and continuing down to the **Refuge du Clot** (3hr 55min), which has full refuge facilities. There is an aire de bivouac above the refuge. Either follow the road down the left-hand side of the river or cross the bridge and follow track and path down the right-hand side. This route passes the bottom station

For a really impressive alternate route through some of the finest scenery in the Pyrenees you could turn right at the Lacs de l'Embarrat, climb hard uphill to the large Lac du Pourtet then descend south down to the Lac Nère and continue downhill to a junction on a pasture then turn left to reach the recently refurbished Refuge Wallon-Marcadau which is staffed year-round. Spend the night here (wonderful riverside camping spots) before following a wild route east to arrive directly at the Refuge des Oulètes de Gaube and the GR10.

An angler in Gave du Marcadau

of the chair lift, which would save you about 200m of climb en route for the Lac de Gaube. Arrive at **Pont d'Espagne** (4hr 10min, 1496m) and rejoin the GR10. ▶

For facilities for this stage, see Stage 18.

STAGE 18

Cauterets to Refuge des Oulètes de Gaube

Start	Cauterets
Distance	15km
Total ascent	1400m
Total descent	100m
Time	6hr 5min
High point	Refuge des Oulètes de Gaube (2151m)

When the GR10 was originally devised it took the easy direct route from Cauterets to Luz-Saint-Sauveur over the Col de Riou. This is described in Stage 18A and it is a route with little merit apart from being quick and easy. Many hikers preferred the spectacular approach to the north face of Vignemale, followed by a crossing of the Houquette d'Ossoue and a descent down to Gavarnie and then north back to Luz-Saint-Sauveur. This alternative route, described here, has been given equal status with the Col de Riou route and it is now seen by most hikers as the main route.

It starts with a climb up the Val de Jéret with its impressive waterfalls followed by an ascent up the Val de Gaube to the Refuge des Oulètes de Gaube with spectacular views of the north wall of Vignemale with its snowfields and remnants of the extensive glaciers that once flowed down the north face. It is a magnificent route, a highlight of the GR10, and so is strongly recommended.

The route over the Col de Riou should only be considered early in the summer when snow could make the crossing of the Hourquette d'Ossoue rather difficult, if bad weather is forecast or you are short of time.

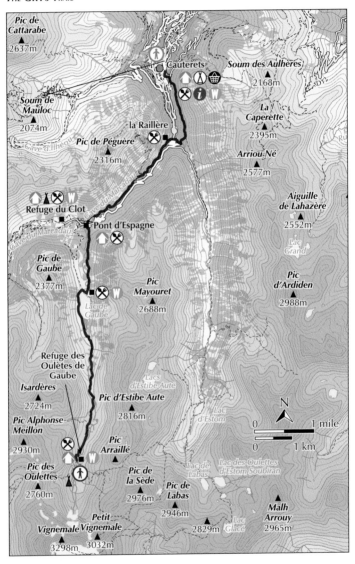

Pic de
Cattarabe
2637m

Cauterets

Soum des Aulhères
2168m

Soum de
Mauloc
2074m

la Raillère

La
Caperette
2395m

Pic de Péguère
2316m

Arriou-Né
2577m

Refuge du Clot

Aiguille
de Lahazère
2552m

Pont d'Espagne

Lac
Grand

Pic de
Gaube
2377m

Pic
Mayouret
2688m

Pic
d'Ardiden
2988m

Lac de
Gaube

Refuge des
Oulètes de
Gaube

Lacs
d'Estibé Aute

Isardères
2724m

Pic d'Estibe Aute
2816m

Lac
d'Estom

N

Pic Alphonse
Meillon
2930m

0   1 mile

0   1 km

Pic
Arraillé

Pic des
Oulettes
2760m

Pic de
la Sède
2976m

Lac de
Labas

Lac des Oulettes
d'Estom Soubiran

Petit
Vignemale
3032m

Pic de
Labas
2946m

Malh
Arrouy
2965m

Vignemale
3298m

2829m

Lac
Glacé

128

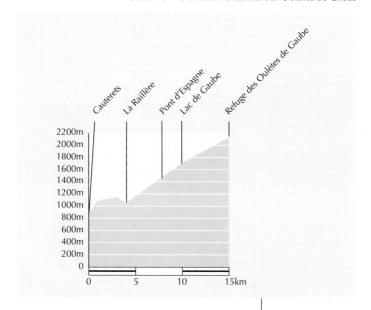

Continue E from the tourist office and go diagonally left up the Allée du Parc to reach les Bains du Rocher and Thermes de César. ▸ Go between the two spa resorts and follow a path behind the Thermes de César. An excellent path zigzags up the hill before going straight across a road. Veer right past a waterpoint and climb gently, high above the river, until you reach a path junction. Fork right and descend to the bridge across the Cascade du Lutour. Cross and fork right to **la Raillère** (1hr 10min, 1044m) with a number of bar-restaurants and souvenir shops. As you approach la Raillère, you will notice a strong sulphurous odour from the natural hot springs which are exploited by the Thermes de Griffons.

The variation of the GR10 via the Col de Riou goes left of les Bains du Rocher.

Cross the bridge over the river and follow the welltrod path up the right-hand side of the Val de Jéret. Pass two bridges and some magnificent waterfalls before turning right up a paved path to reach the Hôtellerie du Pont d'Espagne (2hr 55min, 1496m). ▸

The variation over the Col de la Haugade rejoins the GR10 here (Stage 17A).

Lac de Gaube

The Refuge du Clot, with full refuge facilities and an aire de bivouac, is set in lovely meadows about 10mins up the road to the right of the hotel. There are public toilets and an information office at the huge car park just below the Pont d'Espagne from where there is a shuttle bus service to Cauterets.

Cross the **Pont d'Espagne** and take the road down the right-hand side of the gorge. After 100m turn right up a 'tourist path' and follow this to the **Lac de Gaube** (3hr 50min, 1725m). There is a bar-restaurant with public toilets and a waterpoint at the N tip of the lake. The best swimming is at the S end of the lake.

Head along the W shore of the lake and continue up the right-hand side of the valley before crossing the stream on a bridge. Recross the stream at the next bridge and stay on the right-hand side of the valley at the third bridge. Finally cross the stream to arrive at the popular **Refuge des Oulètes de Gaube** with its magnificent view of the N face of Vignemale (6hr 5min, 2151m). This CAF refuge has full refuge facilities and a waterpoint. The aire de bivouac is on the edge of the meadows on the right-hand side of the valley.

FACILITIES FOR STAGE 18

Hôtellerie du Pont d'Espagne, Pont d'Espagne: tel 05 62 92 54 10, www.hotel-du-pont-despagne.fr

Chalet-refuge du Clot (open June to mid October), Pont d'Espagne: tel 05 62 92 61 27, www.chaletduclot.fr

Refuge des Oulètes de Gaube (open late February to mid October, closed first two weeks of June): tel 09 88 18 41 46, https://refugeoulettesdegaube.ffcam.fr

---

STAGE 18A

Cauterets to Luz-Saint-Sauveur (via Col de Riou)

Start	Cauterets
Distance	22km
Total ascent	1300m
Total descent	1500m
Time	6hr 55min
High point	Col de Riou (1949m)

This easy route was the original direct route of the GR10 from Cauterets to Luz-Saint-Sauveur but, assuming you have time, it is strongly recommended that you follow the magnificent route from Cauterets to Luz-Saint-Sauveur over the Hourquette d'Ossoue as described in Stages 18–20.

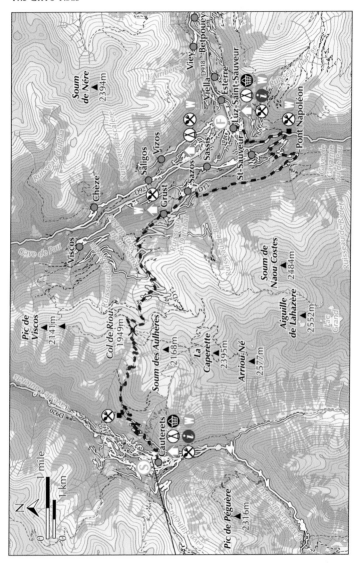

Continue E from the tourist office and go diagonally left up the Allée du Parc to reach les Bains du Rocher. Go to the left of this spa and the fronton, climb the road diagonally right and take a path which climbs right from a bend. Turn left at the second junction, then left and right, cross a stream and turn left along a minor road. This soon becomes a dirt road, which eventually starts zigzagging up to the Reine Hortense bar-restaurant (1hr). The road becomes a forest track and after the first switchback the GR10 goes sharp left up a path. Cross the track when you next meet it, pass a barn in a pasture (1hr 40min) and continue to climb through forest and pasture. The upper pastures provide the first obvious campsites on the ascent. A good path zigzags gently up to the **Col de Riou** (3hr, 1949m) which has good but exposed campsites.

Take the grassy track going diagonally left and fork right along a small path which soon veers right. If you lose the waymarks, which is likely in the confusion of the ski-slopes, follow the yellow-poled ski lift down to le Bédéret bar-café, which is closed in summer. The author has no idea where the waymarks go next. In mist it is probably best to follow the track down but in good

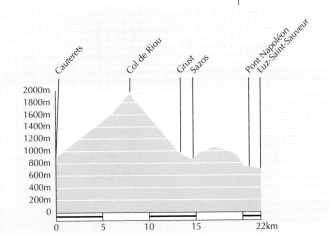

visibility just descend to the top car park of the Luz-Ardiden ski complex. Follow the **D12** road down, taking a lot of waymarked shortcuts, until you reach a sign to Grust at a road crossing (4hr 25min). Follow the path as it zigzags down through the woods, paying careful attention to the waymarks in a maze of paths. The path takes you easily to the small hamlet of **Grust** (4hr 50min, 975m). Pass a waterpoint and the Auberge les Bruyères, then go right at the church and veer left past the Gîte d'étape le Soum de l'Ase and follow the path to the D12.

Descend a little then take a path on the left, which takes you to the hamlet of **Sazos** (5hr 5min, 840m). Turn right past Gîte de Montagne la Maisonnée, right above the church then uphill right at a small square with public toilets. This circuitous route takes you past several waterpoints. Continue up an alley and path to the **D12**. It would be possible to descend this road past Camping Pyrénévasion to Luz-Saint-Sauveur but the GR10 crosses the road and climbs an old cobbled path to reach the Ferme des Cascades where you can purchase cheese. Turn left across the bridge over the waterfall immediately above the farm and follow a good path which roughly contours to reach a roadhead at another farm (5hr 50min). Follow the road, crossing a stream and start descending to reach a junction with the GR10 variation over the Hourquette d'Ossau (6hr). For the continuation of the route to Luz-Saint-Saveur (6hr 55min) refer to Stage 20. ◄

For facilities in Luz-Saint-Sauveur see Stage 20.

FACILITIES FOR STAGE 18A

Grust

Auberge les Bruyères: tel 05 62 92 83 03, www.aubergelesbruyeres.fr

Gîte d'étape le Soum de l'Ase, accommodation and bar-restaurant: tel 05 62 92 34 79, https://sites.google.com/site/soumdelasegite

Sazos

Gîte de Montagne la Maisonnée, accommodation and bar-restaurant: tel 05 62 92 96 90, www.gitelamaisonnee.com

Camping Pyrénévasion, a swish 4-star site: tel 05 62 92 91 54, www.campingpyrenevasion.com

STAGE 19

*Refuge des Oulètes de Gaube to
Chalet-refuge la Grange de Holle*

Start	Refuge des Oulètes de Gaube
Distance	21km
Total ascent	800m
Total descent	1400m
Time	7hr 5min
High point	Hourquette d'Ossoue (2734m)

Although the Hourquette d'Ossoue is the highest pass on the GR10, it is considerably easier in snow than the Hourquette d'Arre (Stage 14). There will be snowfields over the pass well into summer, but the route is well cairned, as well as waymarked, and the path should be easy to follow. There will probably be water on the ascent, depending on the state of snowmelt, but campsites will be in short supply. In good weather you might like to climb Petit Vignemale (3032m). It might be one of the easiest 3000m peaks to climb in the Pyrenees, but that doesn't make the view any less impressive.

The GR10 goes E from the refuge. Fork left after 50m and climb a good rocky path which zigzags up to a junction (1hr 5min). Turn right and climb to the **Hourquette d'Ossoue** (2hr 15min, 2734m). ▶

The path veers left, E, at the col and zigzags down, before reaching a slight climb up a knoll to the **Refuge Baysselance** (2hr 30min, 2651m). The refuge is the normal base for the climb of Vignemale (3298m) by the fast-melting Glacier d'Ossoue; a climb which requires experience and proper mountaineering equipment.

This refuge, the highest manned refuge in the Pyrenees, has full refuge facilities. There is a water-point outside and a rather austere aire de bivouac.

From here you can climb Petit Vignemale, to the right, by its NE ridge – faint paths lead up easy rubble and rock slopes (up and down in 80min).

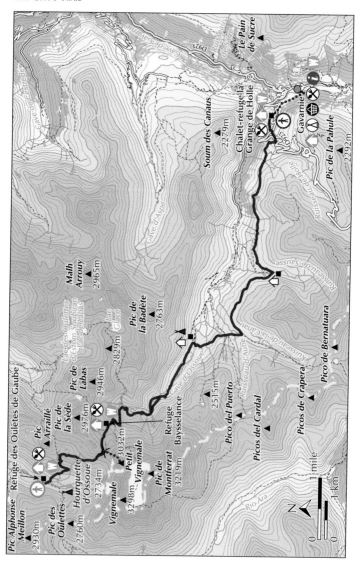

*Vignemale from
Petit Vignemale*

The GR10 continues roughly ESE. The route is easy to follow and surprisingly free of snow by July in an average year. Zigzag down, passing the Grottes de Bellevue (2hr 50min, 2420m).

> The **caves** were hewn out of the rock for Count Henry Russell in the 1880s to provide accommodation for his exploration of Vignemale. They can still be used for an uncomfortable bivouac and are most commonly used by mountaineers climbing the main Vignemale peak.

The path now zigzags steeply down, but surprisingly there are good campsites beside a stream 10mins later. Continue down the good path until you reach a boulderfield through which several meltwater streams from the Glacier d'Ossoue flow. The cairns and waymarking here can be destroyed and may be unclear in mist. You actually gain a little height crossing these boulderfields to pick up the path on the other side. This path climbs slightly as it follows a ledge cut out of the cliffs before continuing the descent; you cannot descend directly down the valley as the stream drops into a series of waterfalls.

As you approach the bottom of the descent you will probably have snowfields to cross well into August. These

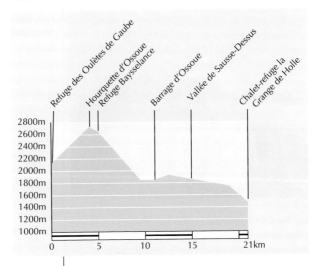

snowfields are the remains of the snow which has ava-
lanched from the cliffs above. Eventually you reach a
bridge across the **Gave d'Ossoue** at the head of the flat
valley floor of the Oulettes d'Ossoue (4hr 5min). Cross
the bridge and follow a vague path down the left-hand
side of the valley to the Barrage d'Ossoue (4hr 25min,
1834m). Swimming possible. There is an aire de bivouac
and a basic bothy by the dam.

The GR10 now follows a generally rising traverse of
the slopes S of the Gave d'Ossoue. There are plenty of
camping opportunities and you cross a number of small
streams. Start by crossing the stream on a bridge immediately below the dam and follow a path roughly S through
pasture, veering SE then S again to pass the Cabane de
Lourdes. Cross the stream flowing from the Vallée de la
Canau on a bridge (5hr), veer left and continue the traverse, passing the Cabane de Sausse-Dessus and crossing
the stream (with rockpool) in the next valley (5hr 35min).
Again, veer left and reach a high point in the traverse (6hr).
There are a few ups and downs before you reach the tiny
Cabane des Tousaus, which could be useful in a storm (6hr

30min). There follows a grassy plateau, at the far end of which the path veers left and follows a little ridge before veering right, down to the **D923** road. Go straight across and across again when you next meet the road to arrive at the **Chalet-refuge la Grange de Holle** (7hr 5min, 1480m).

> Chalet-refuge la Grange de Holle has full refuge facilities and a waterpoint. Camping is possible. There is a good waterhole if you follow the path a few hundred metres down the left side of the stream.

GAVARNIE

The GR10 doesn't actually enter Gavarnie, but you may want to take a day off to visit this car-free village, which is one of the tourist honeypots of the Pyrenees. It has plentiful facilities including bar-restaurants, hotels, gîtes d'étape, campsites (although accommodation can be in very short supply in summer, reserve in advance), a small food shop, tourist office, waterpoint and toilets. There is a bus service to Luz-Saint-Sauveur and on to Lourdes and Tarbes. It's well worth stopping for a day or two in order to enjoy some fantastic day hikes, the most obvious of which is the hike up into the belly of the Cirque de Gavarnie, which claims the highest waterfall in Europe (427m). Rather than follow the standard up-and-back tourist trail take the quiet and more impressive trail to the Plateau de Bellevue (the trail heads off to the right just behind the church) from where you can drop down into the cirque and then return via an easy cliffside path on the opposite side of the valley (this path veers right off main trail behind the restaurant near the head of the cirque). Allow 5hr. Another fantastic route is to climb east of Gavarnie to the Refuge des Espuguettes and from there up to the easy summit of Pimené (2801m) for one of the best viewpoints in the Gavarnie area. Once the snow has melted, it's also possible, and highly recommended, to climb to the renowned Brèche de Roland (2804m), a giant tooth-like gap in the mountain ridge, and on to le Taillon (3146m), which is one of the easiest but most impressive 3000m peaks in the Pyrenees.

FACILITIES FOR STAGE 19

Refuge Baysselance (open mid May to mid October): tel 09 74 77 66 52 or 05 62 92 40 25, http://refugebayssellance.ffcam.fr

Chalet-refuge la Grange de Holle (open May to October): tel 05 62 92 48 77, www.chaletlagrangedeholle.ffcam.fr

Gavarnie

Tourist office: tel 05 62 92 49 10, www.valleesdegavarnie.com

Selected accommodation:

Camping la Bergerie: tel 05 62 92 48 41, www.camping-la-bergerie-gavarnie.com

Gîte d'étape le Gypaète: tel 05 62 92 40 61, http://legypaete.pagesperso-orange.fr

Gîte d'étape Oxygène: tel 05 62 92 48 23, http://gite-gavarnie.com

Hôtel l'Astazou: tel 05 62 95 12 13, hotel.astazou@wanadoo.fr

STAGE 20

*Chalet-refuge la Grange de Holle
to Luz-Saint-Sauveur*

This long stage, which is a generally descending traverse of the west slopes of the Gavarnie Valley, could be split by staying at Gîte d'étape le Saugué.

Start	Chalet-refuge la Grange de Holle
Distance	26km
Total ascent	700m
Total descent	1500m
Time	7hr 45min
High point	NNE ridge of Soum Haut (1874m)

Head down the track from the refuge and almost immediately fork left along a path that follows the wall. The path veers NW and then descends through woods before veering right to cross a bridge over the Gave d'Ossoue (1436m). Follow the path right along the left-hand bank of the river before veering left to cross the road. Go diagonally right, climbing easily to reach the SE ridge

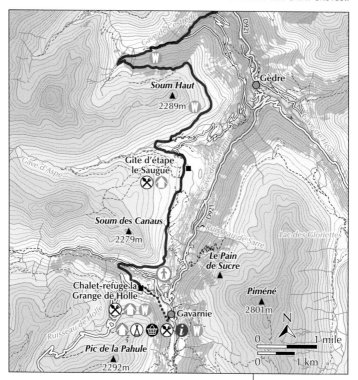

of **Soum des Canaus** (40min, 1563m). Descend below crags then fork left, signed Saugué, and climb to cross a small stream. Follow the path up this stream. The path has become a track by the time it reaches the top of the hill (1hr 15min).

map continues on page 143

The GR10 veers left and right to stay clear of farm buildings before turning right back to the main track and a car park at the roadhead. Keep straight on down the dirt road, which has become a tarmac road by the time you pass the **Gîte d'étape le Saugué** (1hr 40min, 1610m). Three minutes later fork left up a track and right along a path. Keep straight on along tracks above some

141

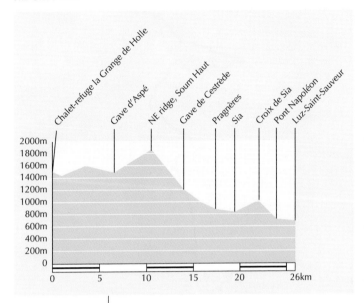

farm buildings to cross a bridge over the **Gave d'Aspé** (1hr 55min). Turn right and start a rising traverse up the S slopes of Soum Haut (2289m). The path isn't always clear, but the waymarking is good and must be followed carefully. As you approach the E ridge of Soum Haut you cross a small spring-fed stream and a few minutes later you can access the spring to the left of the path (2hr 40min). The path levels as it passes left of the highest electricity pylon (1725m). There are good campsites here. You start to descend but then veer left and climb again to reach the NNE ridge of **Soum Haut**, with good campsites (3hr 30min). Climb a little further up the ridge (1874m) before veering right and starting to descend through woods. Cross first one stream then another at the bottom of the forest and continue down the right-hand side of the valley.

Pass a spring-fed waterpoint by a cabin immediately before re-entering the woods (4hr 30min). Cross a dirt road, then cross the **Gave de Cestrède** on the Pont de Balit and continue down the left-hand side of the valley. Veer left at a farm by the road at Trimbareilles (5hr 5min, 1000m). Join the road for a few metres and then veer right down a path, shortcutting the switchbacks in the road. Turn left along the road to reach the **D921** at Pragnères hydro-electric power station (5hr 25min) and turn left. Take care as you descend the busy road. After crossing the **Gave de Gavarnie** on the Pont d'Esdouroucats turn left up a minor road and fork right along a path just before reaching Camping St-Bazerque, a basic campground with café-bar. On returning to the D921, immediately turn left

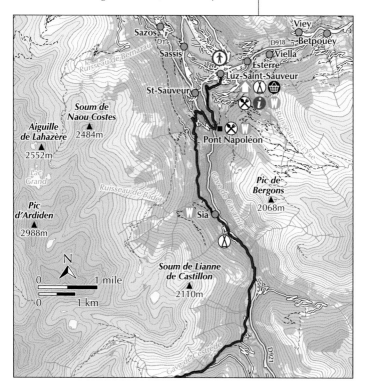

up another minor road, forking right and then right again along a path to return to the D921 at **Sia** (5hr 55min).

The D921 now crosses back to the right-hand side of the valley but the GR10 keeps straight on into Sia, passes a waterpoint and then continues along a good track at the end of the hamlet. When the track bends left, keep straight on up a path crossing a stream and climbing to a path junction. Turn right and follow a path which rises gently through the woods, crossing a stream below a waterfall and continuing to the Croix de Sia at a high point (6hr 45min) where a modern iron cross has replaced the wooden original. Descend to a road (6hr 50min). ◄

This is where the alternative variation of the GR10 described in Stage 18A rejoins from the left.

Shortcut the switchbacks on the road, first to the left, then left and right before following the road downhill. After a right-hand bend, turn sharp left down a track and then, immediately before a stream, right down a path. There is a picnic table across the stream. Descend steeply beside the waterfalls in the stream to reach the road at **St-Sauveur**.

Turn left if you want Hôtel Ardiden, which is just beyond the Thermes Luzéa.

◄ Turn right for the GR10 and pass several hotels to reach **Pont Napoléon** (7hr 20min, 755m), which has a snack bar, toilets, a via ferrata and lots of tourists. Cross the bridge, turn left and follow the road down. Fork right along la Promenade Napoléon III et Eugénie to reach the Chapelle Solférino with picnic tables. Continue along this high-level promenade to arrive at a bridge on the S edge of **Luz-Saint-Sauveur**. The GR10 continues up the right-hand side of the stream, but you will probably want to head N across the bridge to reach the town centre in a few minutes (7hr 45min, 720m).

Luz-Saint-Sauveur is a small and attractive town with all the facilities expected of a tourist resort including two Carrefour supermarkets. There are public toilets behind the tourist office and buses depart from the tourist office for Lourdes, Gavarnie and Cauterets. Gîte d'étape le Regain, Camping Toy, Hôtel Terminus and Hôtel des Cimes are close to the tourist office, as is Intersport, which

stocks all types of camping gas. Gîte d'étape les Cascades, a youth hostel which takes adults, and Camping les Cascades are W of the prominent Église des Templiers.

Chapelle Solférino,
Luz-Saint-Sauveur

FACILITIES FOR STAGE 20

Saugué

Gîte d'étape le Saugué, meals, camping a possibility: tel 05 62 92 48 73, www.gite-gavarnie-pyrenees.com

Sia

Camping St-Bazerque: tel 05 62 92 49 93, www.campingsaintbazerque.eatbu.com

Luz-Saint-Sauveur

Tourist office: tel 05 62 92 30 30, www.luz.org

Selected accommodation:

Gîte d'étape le Regain: tel 05 62 92 92 67, www.gite-leregain.com

Gîte d'étape les Cascades: tel 05 62 92 94 14, www.camping-luz.fr

Hôtel Ardiden: tel 05 62 92 81 80, www.hotelardiden.com

Hôtel Terminus: tel 05 62 92 80 17, www.luz-terminus.fr

Hôtel des Cimes: tel 05 62 92 81 52

Camping les Cascades: tel 05 62 92 85 85, www.camping-luz.fr

Camping Toy: tel 05 62 92 86 85, www.camping-toy.com

STAGE 21
Luz-Saint-Sauveur to Barèges

Start	Luz-Saint-Sauveur
Distance	12km
Total ascent	800m
Total descent	300m
Time	4hr 30min
High point	Ruisseau de Bolou (1460m)

This short stage starts with a long and very steep climb before traversing the south slopes of the Bastan Valley to Barèges.

Return to the bridge on the south edge of Luz-Saint-Sauveur and climb up the right-hand side of the stream. At Villenave go left across the bridge and immediately right (waterpoint to the left) and left along a path. Veer uphill right at a complex junction and climb steeply to a path junction (45min, 990m). ◄

The left turn takes you down to Viella.

The GR10 goes right and continues to climb steeply through the wood before veering left and reaching the NW ridge of **Soum de la Courbe** (1hr 55min, 1322m). Descend a little through clumps of wild raspberry

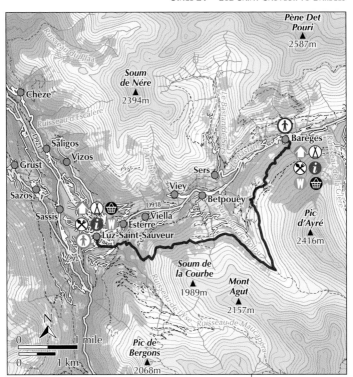

bushes, then fork right at a junction and turn left to reach the first camping opportunity on the ascent in a tiny meadow (2hr 10min). Pick up a grassy track here, then fork right at a gate and turn sharp right just before a barn and climb steeply. Immediately after crossing an electric fence, turn left and descend. The path soon levels and you cross three small streams in quick succession (2hr 40min). This is the first water on the ascent, but the water quality is questionable. Contour, then pass left through an electric fence and continue contouring to the Gué de Bolou (3hr 15min, 1460m). This stream could be difficult to cross when it is in flood, but

Looking down the valley of the Ruisseau de Bolou

it emerges from underground a short distance upstream for a dry foot crossing. Also head upstream if you are wanting to camp.

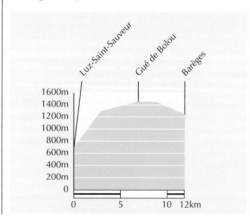

The GR10 continues to contour until you approach power lines where you fork left and descend to a small tarmac road (3hr 50min). Turn right. Ignore a left turn and right fork, then fork right twice and fork left along a contouring path. You soon fork left to start the easy descent through woods to Barèges. Ignore turns and cross several streams before arriving at les Thermes de Barèges in **Barèges** (4hr 30min, 1240m).

Barèges is a small winter ski resort and in summer is used by hikers and cyclists. There is an Intersport, which sells all types of camping gas, and a waterpoint at the junction with les Thermes de Barèges. Most of the facilities, including the tourist office, are down the main road to the left.

FACILITIES FOR STAGE 21

Viella

Gîte d'étape la Grange au Bois: tel 05 62 92 93 84, www.lagrangeaubois.fr

Barèges

Tourist office: tel 05 62 92 16 00, www.grand-tourmalet.com

Selected accommodation:

Gîte d'étape l'Oasis: tel 05 62 92 69 47, www.gite-oasis.fr

Hôtel les Sorbiers (English owners): tel 05 62 96 7740, www.les-sorbiers.com

Hôtel la Montagne Fleurie: tel 05 62 92 68 50, www.montagnefleurie.fr

Camping la Ribère: tel 05 62 92 69 01, www.laribere.fr

STAGE 22

Barèges to Refuge-Hôtel de l'Oule

Start	Barèges
Distance	23km
Total ascent	1300m
Total descent	700m
Time	7hr 45min; alternative route 8hr 45min
High point	Col de Madamète (2509m)

This long stage – through the heart of the lake-spotted Néouvielle region – crosses the Col de Madamète, which is remarkably easy for such a high pass. This is a long walk through beautiful countryside where there's always the temptation to lounge lakeside. Because of this few people would regret breaking this section down into two shorter but more enjoyable days. There are plentiful camping spots and the new Refuge d'Aygues Cluses or the Chalet-Hôtel d'Orédon at the east end of Lac d'Orédon are also both great places to break for the night.

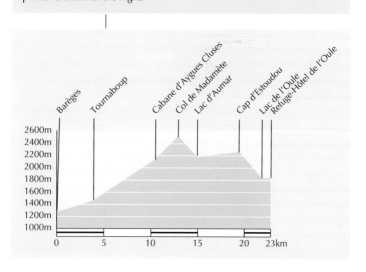

Head up the main road, passing the Gîte d'étape l'Oasis and turn left across the bridge over Le Bastan. Turn right alongside the river then climb a grassy bank to reach a small tarmac road. Turn left then right and follow the road as it climbs. At a switchback, keep straight on up a grassy track, which becomes a path that veers left up to a track. Turn right and pass through magnificent wildflower meadows. Cross a couple of streams then fork right just after a farm (40min) and descend to cross a bridge over the river. Turn left and follow the track to the **D918**. Turn left and follow the left-hand road past a snack bar and Auberge la Couquelle ▶ to the bridge at the **Tournaboup** ski area (1hr). The bar-restaurant/snack bar and chair lift at the ski area are open in the summer.

The Auberge la Couquelle is a bar-restaurant that offers accommodation.

You are now at the foot of the road pass over the **Col du Tourmalet**, which has been made famous by frequent use in the Tour de France. There seems to be a continuous flow of cyclists climbing to or descending from the col.

Map continues on page 152

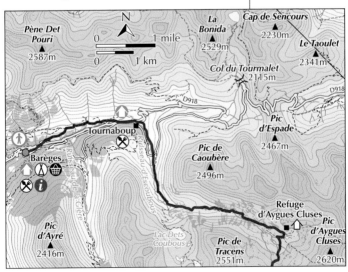

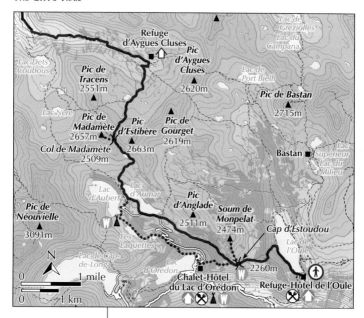

An alternative route, the GR10C (not described in this guide), continues up the D918.

The GR10 turns right and climbs to the left of the Coubous stream. ◄ The waymarking may not be clear but you stay left of the wood to reach the old road (1hr 20min, 1538m). Go straight across and continue up the left-hand side of the valley, joining a track. Eventually cross the stream and reach a path junction (2hr). Turn left and follow a clear stony path. You are back into a typical granite landscape, which provides magnificent scenery. The stream disappears underground for some time and there are good campsites in the meadows where it reappears (2hr 35min). There are many strands to the path, with the GR10 waymarked to avoid the meadows while most tourists use the old paths through the meadows. You cross the stream several times before eventually reaching the new and very stylish **Refuge d'Aygues Cluses** (3hr 35min, 2150m) by the shallow Lac de Coueyla-Gran. This new refuge is replacing the old stone cabin that provided simple accommodation for many years.

Looking southeast from Pic de Madamète

If you want to break this stage up then this is a good place to stop. There's dorm accommodation and meals available in the refuge and some lovely lakeside camping spots. ▶

Continuing onwards, the GR10 switches back right before veering S then SW and crossing several streams before passing between the two Lacs de Madamète (swimming possible) (4hr 5min). As usual when crossing high passes the waymarks get scarcer, to be replaced by cairns, but the path remains very obvious. Continue roughly SSW, passing left of two shallow tarns and left of a possibly ice-bound lake to reach the **Col de Madamète** (4hr 55min, 2509m). Expect snow on the lead up to the pass until at least mid June. ▶

There have been camping opportunities and water throughout the ascent, but you are now entering la Réserve Naturelle de Néouvielle where camping

A moderate walk to the summit of Pic d'Aygues Cluses (2620m) is possible via the Hourquette Nère and descending via the Col de Barèges (allow 3hr).

Pic de Madamète (2657m) to the right is an easy peak with a cairned path to the summit (there and back in 25min).

is restricted to the aire de bivouac below the Lac d'Aubert dam and at Lac d'Orédon, as described in the alternative route from Lac d'Aumar. Apart from these sites, the next legal wild camping is at the N end of Lac de l'Oule in Stage 23.

Head straight down the other side, passing left of the Gourg de Rabas (swimming possible), on boulderfield. Shortly afterwards veer right, SW, and then left to reach the NW end of **Lac d'Aumar** (5hr 35min, 2190m), which is popular with tourists as it is accessed by a shuttle bus service. ◄ Continue along the S shore of the lake and, after a few minutes, pass a sign to the aire de bivouac.

There is excellent swimming from the NW shore.

Alternative route via Lac d'Orédon

If you want to camp, or if you require the Chalet-Hôtel d'Orédon, you should turn right and descend to the aire de bivouac immediately below the dam of **Lac d'Aubert** (5hr 50min, 2148m) where there are toilets and a waterpoint. You can either return to the GR10 or descend, following the cairned path from the aire de bivouac. Pass along the N shore of les Laquettes and turn right immediately before reaching a road. Stay on the path when you next meet the road and arrive at the aire de bivouac at the E end of **Lac d'Orèdon** (6hr 45min, 1856m) with information office, toilets, a waterpoint and good swimming.

Go a short distance along the road and turn left, steeply uphill, by the Refuge du Lac, which is part of the **Chalet-Hôtel du Lac d'Orèdon**, which you soon reach. Turn left up the road and soon fork right up a steep, well-trod but unwaymarked path to reach a junction with the GR10 at a good spring just below the **Cap d'Estoudou** (8hr).

There is an easy ascent of the Soum de Monpelat (2474m) to the left (a return journey will take 55min).

Ignore the road as you continue along the shore to the SE end of the lake. Keep straight on along a grassy plateau and then climb a little before descending to a small ridge and following a descending traverse before the final ascent to the **Cap d'Estoudou** (7hr, 2260m). There is a spring just before you reach the col. ◄

Descend steeply on the clear path to reach the **Lac de l'Oule** (7hr 35min, 1821m). If you don't want the refuge you can turn left and start Stage 23. Turn right for the **Refuge-Hôtel de l'Oule**, with full refuge facilities, at the E end of the dam at the S end of the lake (7hr 45min).

FACILITIES FOR STAGE 22

Tournaboup

Auberge la Couquelle: tel 05 62 92 68 15, lacouquelle@wanadoo.fr

Refuge d'Aygues Cluses (open June to September): contact details unknown at time of research

Lac d'Orédon

Chalet-Hôtel du Lac d'Orédon, refuge or hotel accommodation (open June to September): tel 06 38 25 96 42, www.chalet-oredon.fr

Lac de l'Oule

Refuge-Hôtel de l'Oule (open mid June to mid September): tel 05 62 98 48 62, www.saintlary-vacances.com/oule

STAGE 23
Refuge-Hôtel de l'Oule to Vielle-Aure

Start	Refuge-Hôtel de l'Oule
Distance	17km
Total ascent	400m
Total descent	1400m
Time	4hr 40min
High point	Col de Portet (2215m)

This is an easy stage climbing over the grassy Col de Portet, which is unfortunately rather despoiled by ski slopes. Camping is possible throughout the section until the final steep descent.

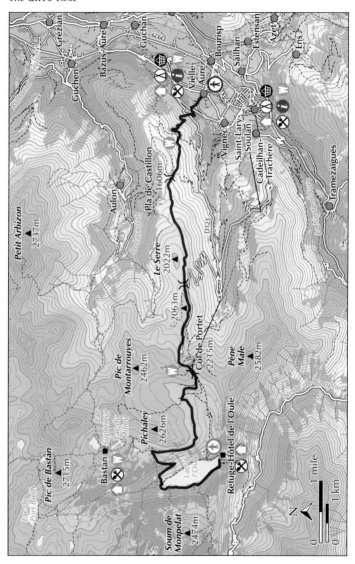

Return to the junction on the W shore of Lac de l'Oule and pass an old stone cabin, which could be used for a very rough bivouac. Continue to the bridge at the N end of the lake (swimming possible) (30min). The campsites here are the first legal sites since the Col de Madamète. Cross the bridge and climb ENE to the right of the Bastan stream and climb past the Cabane de Bastan to a junction with the GR10C (1hr 25min, 2110m). ▶

The GR10 switches back right and traverses grassy pasture along the W slopes of **Pichaley**. Ignore a right fork and follow the path as it veers left to pass under ski lifts on the S slopes of the mountain. Ignore a multitude of animal tracks and tracks associated with the ski slopes. Cross two small streams (2hr 5min) and fork right to contour round the S ridge of **Pic de Montarrouyes** and climb easily alongside a chair lift to the **Col de Portet** (2hr 20min, 2215m) with car parking and ski lifts.

The GR10 veers left down a ski piste, soon forking left along a gently descending path and passing just above a good spring. Ignore animal tracks contouring off to the left as you descend parallel to the road. After you have

Lac de l'Oule

The Refuge de Bastan is about 30min left along the GR10C surrounded by some lovely lakes.

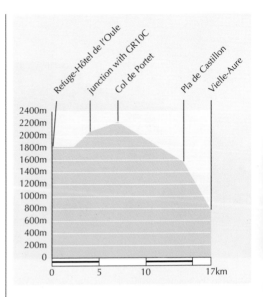

left the ski slopes behind, the GR10 starts to contour the S slopes of Peak 2063 to reach a track at a col (2hr 55min). Continue along the track, passing right of a cattle pen and then pick up the path which contours the S slopes of **Le Serre** before descending its grassy E ridge to a gate. You soon fork right, not clearly waymarked, to arrive at a col (3hr 35min, 1606m) with signpost at the Pla de Castillon.

Veer right and follow the fence down to a waterpoint (3hr 50min), which can be unreliable in a very dry summer. There is poor waymarking here, but the GR10 follows the good track down before going straight on along a path into the woods at a switchback in the track. This path zigzags easily down the steep slope. There are a few nebulous path junctions at which you take the descending option. When you reach the **D123** road (4hr 20min), go straight across. You also go straight across when you next meet the D123, descending to the right of a car park.

You soon pass the entrance to the Mines de Vielle-Aure. ◄ Continue descending down a tarmac road to

These ancient manganese mines have been renovated as a tourist attraction.

arrive at the central square in the small village of **Vielle-Aure** (4hr 40min, 800m).

> The tourist office and a bar-restaurant are in the square. Hôtel Aurélia is W along the D19 on the S side of the river. The large Carrefour supermarket, which is on your right as you walk from Vielle-Aure to Bourisp, stocks all types of camping gas. There is a wide choice of campgrounds. The Camping la Mousquère is on the GR10 on the way into Bourisp or Camping Municipal is in the centre of St-Lary-Soulan. There is a bus service from Vielle-Aure to Tarbes via Lannemezan, connecting with the French rail network. In July/August there is a bus service to Loudenvielle.

Saint-Lary-Soulan, to the S, is a major ski and tourist resort with a much wider range of facilities for the hiker.

FACILITIES FOR STAGE 23

Bastan

Refuge du Bastan (open late May to late October): tel 09 74 76 64 65, http://refugedebastan.fr

Vielle-Aure and Bourisp

Tourist office: 05 62 39 50 00, www.vielleaure.com

Hôtel Aurélia: tel 05 62 39 56 90, www.hotel-aurelia.com

Camping la Mousquère: tel 05 62 39 44 99, www.campinglamousquere.com

Saint-Lary-Soulan

Tourist office: tel 08 25 86 50 65, www.saintlary.com

Selected accommodation:

Hôtel d'Orédon: tel 05 62 39 40 04, www.saint-lary-hotel.com

Hôtel Mir: tel 05 62 39 40 46, https://hotelmir.fr

Gîte le refuge à Saint-Lary-Soulan, mainly takes groups but may be able to cater for GR10 hikers: tel 05 62 39 46 81, www.adhoc-pyrenees.fr

Camping Municipal Lallane: tel 05 62 39 41 58

STAGE 24

Vielle-Aure to Germ

Start	Vielle-Aure
Distance	13km
Total ascent	1200m
Total descent	700m
Time	4hr 35min
High point	Above Col d'Azet (1600m)

This easy stage parallels the D225 as it climbs over a low pass to descend to Loudenvielle. The path isn't always clear or well waymarked so care will be needed with route finding.

Keep straight on across the bridge over the Neste d'Aure. Public toilets with water are just ahead. The GR10 turns left alongside the river, then right after 100m to follow the old road. Veer right as this peters out to return to the D116 by the Carrefour supermarket. Turn left and

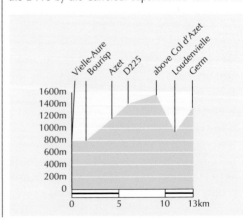

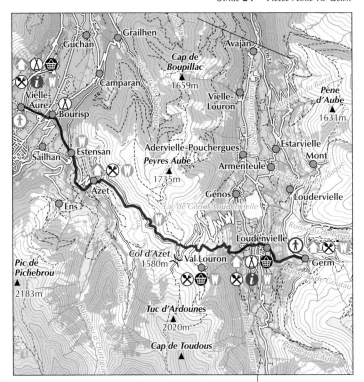

go across the roundabout, passing the campground Camping la Mousquère then turning left across a bridge into the small village of **Bourisp** (800m).

After 50m, turn right up a steep alley and turn right along a track, which winds up the hill and becomes a path, which you follow to **Estensan** (45min). Keep straight on past the church with a waterpoint. At the end of the hamlet fork right, signed Estensagnet, passing more waterpoints. Fork left up a track at the end of Estensagnet. On meeting the D225 go round the switchback and then fork right up a track. On reaching **Azet**, turn right to reach the church with a waterpoint (1hr 15min, 1168m). Gîte d'étape le Bergerie is 50m downhill on the right and there are several chambres d'hôtes.

At the church, fork left up the D225 then right up a path. Turn right, fork left and then veer right for a gentle ascending traverse to return to the D225 (2hr). Go straight across the road. The path now gets less well defined, but it continues as a rising traverse left of a fence, passing a waterpoint before veering away from the fence and left round a small ridge. As you approach the main ridge, the road veers S to the Col d'Azet, but the GR10 continues roughly ESE to reach a track on the ridge about 500m N of the **Col d'Azet** (2hr 40min, 1600m).

Go straight across the track, or find the start of the descent if you have lost the trail, and start descending along nebulous paths. Go straight across the D225 and the access road to the ski resort of **Val Louron**. ◄

The GR10 doesn't go through the resort but there is a bar-restaurant and small shop (should be open in July and August) as well as toilets and a waterpoint.

Continue down, passing right of a cattle pen, and follow a well-waymarked but complex route, eventually finding a path which zigzags down the lower slopes to arrive at **Loudenvielle**. Pass a picnic site and Camping de Pène Blanche before keeping straight on to the centre of the village to arrive at the tourist office (3hr 35min, 970m).

At Loudenvielle there are shops, including a small Carrefour supermarket, bar-restaurants and toilets near the tourist office. Accommodation is very limited.

Keep straight on passing several waterpoints. Veer right, turn left before the church, veer right and then fork left to start the steep climb to **Germ** (4hr 35min, 1339m) which has a gîte d'étape and auberge.

A flower-festooned waterpoint in Germ

FACILITIES FOR STAGE 24

Azet

Gîte d'étape le Bergerie, chambres d'hôtes, gîte d'étape accommodation and full meals: tel 05 62 39 49 49, www.labergerie-azet.fr

Loudenvielle

Tourist office: 05 62 99 95 35, www.vallee-du-louron.com

Wellness Sport Camping: tel 05 62 99 68 85,
https://loudenvielle.wellness-sport-camping.com

Chambres d'hôtes les Noisetiers: tel 06 20 70 12 40,
www.noisetiers-pyrenees.com

Germ

Centre de Montagne de Germ, gîte d'étape, aire de bivouac and swimming pool: tel 05 62 99 65 27, www.germ-louron.com

Auberge de Germ: tel 05 62 40 03 97, www.auberge-de-germ.fr

STAGE 25

Germ to Lac d'Oô

Start	Germ
Distance	16km
Total ascent	1200m
Total descent	1000m
Time	6hr
High points	Couret d'Esquierry (2131m), Lac d'Oô (1504m)

The GR10 now returns to the high mountains for a crossing of the Couret d'Esquierry. Stages 25 and 26 are both tough days and it would be possible to break into three days by staying at Granges d'Astau and the Refuge d'Espingo.

Keep straight on through Germ, passing several water-points, public toilets and the Auberge de Germ. After

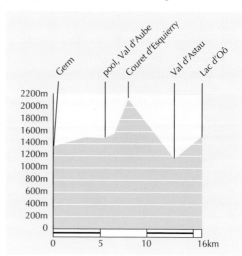

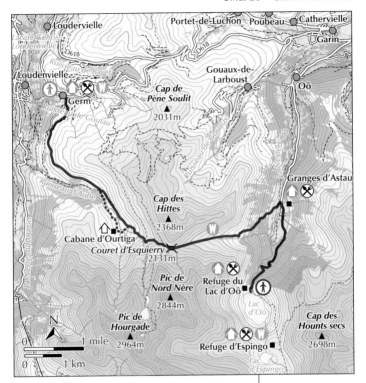

about 200m, fork left and climb steeply up a track
before forking right and traversing. Fork left up a path
on a generally rising traverse. After a high point, enter
the Val d'Aube. A slight descent takes you down to the
floor of the valley at a small dam (cold swimming) (1hr
5min, 1487m). If you want the Cabane d'Ourtiga, a hut
in good condition, you should follow the paths on the
right-hand side of the stream. The GR10 continues up
the left-hand side to reach flatter pasture, with good
campsites, across the stream from the hut (1hr 35min,
1620m).

West from Couret d'Esquierry

A path leads right from the col to the Lacs de Nère and Pic de Hourgade (2964m), a rather challenging scramble that should only be done by the sure of foot on a clear day.

The GR10 now veers slightly left to reach the left-hand stream descending from above. Cross this stream and climb a small, but easily followed, steep path which climbs the ridge to the right of the stream. The only water is early on the climb. The ascent is too steep for camping but it would be possible to camp when you arrive at the grassy **Couret d'Esquierry** (3hr 15min, 2131m). ◄

Keep straight on and descend the dry valley, eventually reaching a good spring to your left. The GR10 now veers right to reach a shepherd's hut, the Cabane du Val d'Esquierry (3hr 55min). Descend left from here, cross the stream, descend a grassy shoulder and enter the woods. The path then zigzags down steep slopes to a farm in the Val d'Astau. Follow the tarmac farm road to the bridge over the river, cross and turn right up the D76 to reach **Granges d'Astau** and the Auberge d'Astau (4hr 45min, 1139m).

In July and August, there is a morning and evening bus service from the large car park to Bagnères-de-Luchon. There is a bar-restaurant here and it should be possible to camp on the right above Granges d'Astau, after which the next obvious camping is in the vicinity of the Refuge d'Espingo or on the descent from the Hourquette des Hounts-Secs.

Join the day trip masses on the track up the valley. Ignore two paths going off right before arriving at the bridge just below the **Lac d'Oô dam**. If you don't need the Refuge du Lac d'Oô, go straight on and start Stage 26. Otherwise cross the bridge and arrive at the **Refuge du Lac d'Oô** with full refuge facilities (6hr, 1504m). No camping or swimming! ▸

The spectacular waterfall across the reservoir is the Cascade d' Oô.

FACILITIES FOR STAGE 25

Granges d'Astau

Auberge d'Astau, chambres d'hôtes, gîte d'étape accommodation and bar-restaurant: tel 05 61 95 30 16, https://astau.fr

Lac d'Oô

Refuge du Lac d'Oô (open May to October): tel 07 84 56 55 88, https://refuge-du-lac-doo.business.site

STAGE 26
Lac d'Oô to Bagnères-de-Luchon

Start	Lac d'Oô
Distance	19km
Total ascent	1000m
Total descent	1900m
Time	7hr
High point	Hourquette des Hounts-Secs (2275m), Col de la Coume de Bourg (2272m)

This long stage could be broken by staying at the Refuge d'Espingo. The going could be tough on this high-level traverse, especially in bad weather or in early season when snow could linger on the north-facing slopes between the Hourquette des Hounts-Secs and Col de la Coume de Bourg. The day ends with a long descent down to Bagnères-de-Luchon.

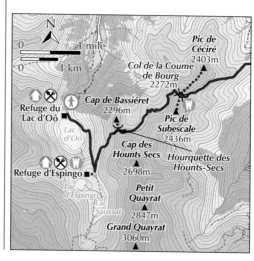

Map continues on page 170

Lac d'Espingo

Return to the bridge and climb to the left-hand end of the dam. The path soon climbs high above the E shore of the reservoir before continuing on a rising traverse. Cross two streams just below cascading waterfalls and follow the path up a valley to a path junction by a big boulder (1hr 30min).

> The main path continues up the valley and reaches the Refuge d'Espingo, which has full refuge facilities and a waterpoint, in 10mins. Lac d'Espingo, below the refuge, is popular with campers and has good swimming.

The GR10 switches back left up a small but clear path. You cross a stream, which may be your last water until the small spring on the other side of the Col de la Coume de Bourg. The path zigzags easily up to the **Hourquette des Hounts-Secs** (2hr 50min, 2275m). ▶

Cap de Bassiéret (2296m), to the left, is a very easy scramble (up and down in 15min).

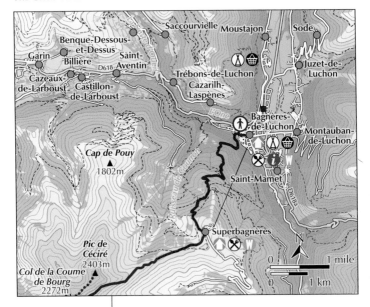

The path descends right, veering left along the N slopes of **Caps de Hounts-Secs** (2513m), with good campsites, before climbing over the NW ridges of Pic de Coume Nére and **Pic de Subescale** and climbing switchbacks to the **Col de la Coume de Bourg** (4hr 15min, 2272m).

From this col there is a path leading left, bypassing the Sommet de la Coume de Bourg (2347m), to reach **Pic de Cécíré** (2403m) to the northeast (return journey of 45 minutes). **Pic de Subescale** (2436m) to the southwest can be climbed on sheep tracks (there and back in 40 minutes).

There is a profusion of animal tracks here, but the GR10 descends and, in a few minutes, passes a spring-fed pipe protected by a cairn of boulders. When Superbagnères is closed this will be your last water before Luchon! Camping possible.

The path veers left and traverses the steep craggy S slopes of Pic de Céciré, eventually reaching its E ridge under some powerlines (5hr). Continue along the crest of the ridge to the top of the chair lift. The waymarking through the ski area is rather sparse, but veer slightly left, then turn left along a track to reach the **Superbagnères** ski complex (5hr 20min, 1804m). The facilities, including the bar-restaurant, toilets with water and hotel, are only open in July and August.

Take the track left of the resort, forking left then crossing a ski piste to arrive at a derelict hexagonal shelter and picnic table. Go diagonally left here, through meadow and into the woods. Fork left and zigzag down the steep slope. Turn right at a forest road (5hr 50min) and fork left down a grassy track. Turn left down a path and switchback down. Cross a track and then rejoin the track. This is the best place to camp if you want to stop before Luchon (6hr 15min). Almost immediately turn right and

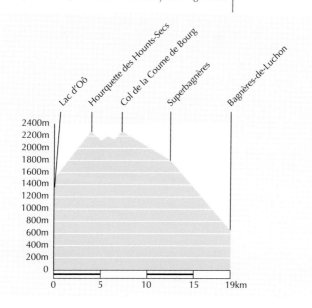

zigzag down, eventually reaching a junction where you turn left. Pass the Source Palo del Mailh, which is probably just running and, a few minutes later, reach the top of **Bagnères-de-Luchon**. Descend a narrow tarmac road, turn left and right past the market square to reach a church (7hr, 650m).

Bagnères-de-Luchon is a small and attractive town that attracts lots of visitors. Most of the facilities, including the tourist office and waterpoint, are to the right. Intersport, by the tourist office, stocks Coleman-style camping gas. Turn left for the railway station.

FACILITIES FOR STAGE 26

Refuge d'Espingo (open mid May to mid October): tel 09 88 66 99 69, http://refugedespingo.ffcam.fr

Superbagnères

Hôtel Superbagnères, part of les Villages Clubs du Soleil, mainly for longer holidays but an overnight stay may be possible during July and August: tel 05 61 79 90 00

Bagnères-de-Luchon

Tourist office: tel 05 61 79 21 21, www.pyrenees31.com

A small selection of the available facilities:

Camping au fil de l'Oô: tel 05 61 79 30 74, http://campingaufildeloo.com

Camping Pradelongue: tel 05 61 79 86 44, www.camping-pradelongue.com

Hôtel la Rencluse: tel 05 61 9591 23, www.hotel-larencluse.com

Gîte le Lutin: tel 05 61 89 70 86, http://gite-luchon-pyrenees.fr

3 BAGNÈRES-DE-LUCHON TO MÉRENS-LES-VALS

KEY INFORMATION

Distance	265km
Total ascent	17,600m
Time	99hr walking
Maps	IGN Carte de Randonnées 1:50,000 maps 5–7

The border between France and Spain is well north of the watershed in this section and the GR10 passes through the Ariège. These mountains aren't quite as high as the High Pyrenees, but the valleys running north from the watershed are deeper and the slopes are steeper meaning that there is a lot of climbing. The Ariège has never been as popular a visitor destination as the High Pyrenees and there is often a feeling of remoteness to the region and facilities for walkers can be harder to find. However, this also means that an older lifestyle survives here. Hill farming and transhumance livestock herding still survive and this lends an interesting cultural depth to your time in the Ariège.

On the approach to Col d'Auéran (Stage 29)

STAGE 27

Bagnères-de-Luchon to Artigue

Start	Bagnères-de-Luchon
Distance	8km
Total ascent	600m
Total descent	0m
Time	2hr 35min
High point	Artigue (1230m)

This is not much more than a rest day. Older editions of this guide went straight through from Bagnères-de-Luchon to Fos but that left a stage that was too long for the average hiker.

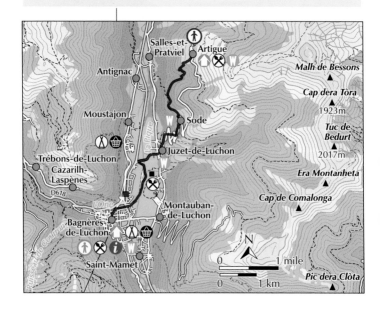

Turn left, NE, at the church in Bagnères-de-Luchon and then veer right down Avenue Marechal Foch. Turn right at the Casino supermarket. Follow a path to the right of the river, cross a road bridge and follow the cycle track along the left-hand bank, passing an aire de camping-car with a waterpoint. Continue alongside the airfield, which is used for gliders and light aircraft. When the path forks left alongside the airfield, continue along the cycle path past picnic sites and a bar-restaurant. Veer left along a road at the end of the airfield to the back of the Mr Bricolage store (25min).

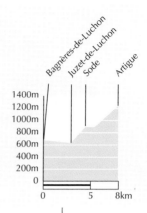

If you want the big Intermarché supermarket, continue left to the roundabout. The store, which sells all types of camping gas, is a short distance diagonally right, beside Camping Pradelongue. Unfortunately, to reach it you need to turn right then left and left again (about 15min).

The GR10 turns right up the D46 and follows it into and through **Juzet-de-Luchon**. ▶

Pass a waterpoint then veer left, turn right up the road to Sode and fork right up some steps (40min). The climb now starts in earnest and the D46 is crossed five times. At the sixth meeting, turn left to an inconsistent waterpoint on the edge of **Sode** (1hr 25min). There are a few possible campsites between Sode and Artigue. Fork left and the follow waymarks carefully as you wind through the hamlet to exit along a path contouring into the woods. Fork right, then follow the main path on an undulating traverse before crossing a trickling stream (1hr 55min) and zigzagging up the steep slope. Pass an old stone shelter, which could be used in an emergency, and continue to reach the waterpoint in **Artigue** (2hr 35min, 1230m).

There are signs to la Cascade in Juzet; this dramatic waterfall is only a few minutes upstream and it is even possible for the daring to have a bracing shower.

*An old barn
in Artigue*

The Gîte d'étape d'Artigue is to the right, the chambres d'hôtes ahead and the restaurant is at the top right of the hamlet. The gîte d'étape has a kitchen but does not provide meals, so you might like to book your evening meal at the restaurant. Picnic lunches may be possible.

FACILITIES FOR STAGE 27

Artigue

Gîte d'étape d'Artigue: tel 06 77 23 37 48, https://artigue31110.wordpress.com

Chambres d'hôtes Eth Artigaou: tel 06 82 44 02 25, www.artigaou.fr

Restaurant les Hauts Pâturages: tel 05 61 79 10 47

STAGE 28

Artigue to Fos

Start	Artigue
Distance	21km
Total ascent	1100m
Total descent	1800m
Time	6hr 50min
High point	Pic de Bacanère (2193m)

This stage crosses the Pic de Bacanère on easy grass ridges. Being on open ridges, you will be exposed to the elements in bad weather.

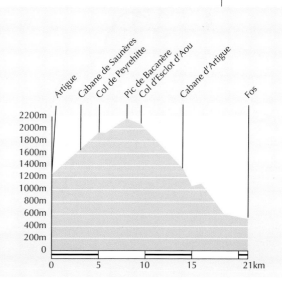

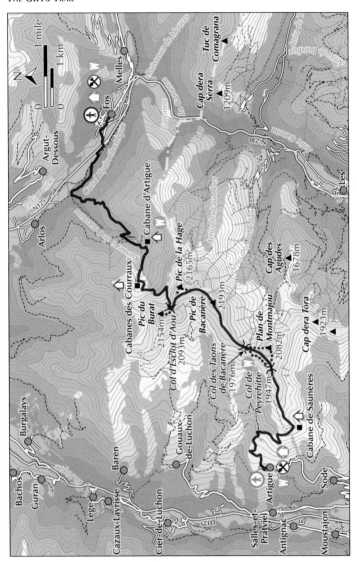

Keep straight on, N, along the lower road, turning right at the church and veering left up a tarmac farm road. Ignore two right turns as the road becomes a track and climb through hayfields before forking right into the forest. Go right and right again. When you meet a forest road, veer left and switch back right up a track and onto open hillside (45min). The track zigzags to reach the **Cabane de Saunères** (1hr 10min, 1660m), a lovely stone cabin which is in excellent condition and quite well equipped. There are exposed campsites here and throughout the remainder of the ascent.

A bothy with a view, Cabane de Saunères

Turn left, uphill, and follow a small path that crosses the ridge. Continue climbing to the left of the rocky Serrat de Créspés (1888m) and emerge on a broad grassy ridge (1hr 50min). Follow it past a tiny wooden hut (one-man bothy?) to the **Col de Peyrehitte** (2hr 5min, 1947m). ▶

The GR10 veers left and traverses the NW slopes of the **Plan de Montmajou** on a path above a grassy track.

In good weather you might like to keep straight on up the Plan de Montmajou (2082m), rejoining the GR10 by descending its N ridge.

You could follow the track that leads to a small spring, veering right and climbing back to the GR10. This is the only water on the ascent and possibly the only water you could drink without treating before Fos.

Notice how far N the border is from the watershed. You can see Aneto (3404m), the highest peak in the Pyrenees, to the S.

The GR10 regains the ridge at the **Col des Taons de Bacanère** (1967m) where there are some ruins. You are now on the French-Spanish border and pass borderstones 398, 399 and 400 as you follow the ridge to **Pic de Bacanère** (2hr 55min, 2193m) with borderstone 401. ◄

In good weather you could climb this peak and regain the GR10 by its NW ridge.

The GR10 veers left past borderstones 402 and 403 to a col with a pond and borderstone 404 (3hr 5min). Veer left, passing borderstone 405 on a small top and then veer left again to traverse the SW slopes of **Pic de la Hage**. ◄ The GR10 gains the NW ridge and soon reaches the Col d'Esclot d'Aou (3hr 25min, 2093m). Pic de Burat (2154m) ahead is an easy climb (up and down in 20min).

Fork right down a small well-waymarked path and continue down to the two huts of the **Cabanes des Courraux** (4hr 15min, 1586m).

Shepherds use both this and the Cabane d'Artigue, ahead, during the summer, although there's often space in one or the other for walkers and the shepherds extend a warm welcome. Either site would provide good campsites if the cows are elsewhere.

Descend between the two huts and cross a stream. The water looks good but it does come from the pastures above. Roughly contour to the **Cabane d'Artigue** at the W end of more meadows (4hr 40min). There's a spring here.

The path soon switches back left, back into the forest. Cross a stream, turn right, fork right, cross a track and then keep straight on down a path to the left of the stream. Go straight across a track then left along the next track and switch back right down a good path (5hr 5min). The GR10 used to go straight on here, but the steep descent down the Ruisseau de Batch is considered dangerous and only recommended in ascent. Cross a stream, possibly your last water on the descent, and climb steadily along a good path, ignoring a left fork. When the path has levelled off (5hr 30min), fork left and start the descent, which is actually quite gentle as it involves around 54 switchbacks. Surprisingly there are quite a few places on the descent where camping would be possible.

Eventually you will arrive at some ruins just above the stream (6hr 10min). Turn right and climb above some crags before completing the descent to a **canal**, which is part of an EDF hydro-electric scheme (6hr 30min). Turn right, then left across the canal to reach a roundabout. Go straight across, signed to Fos, then turn left along the Chemin d'Arné, passing the first of many waterpoints in Fos. Return to the main road by the bridge over **La Garonne** (544m). Keep straight on for the hotel and boulangerie. The GR10 crosses the bridge and goes sharp left to reach the Gîte d'étape de Fos (6hr 50min), although at the time of writing it was uncertain if this place was going to remain open.

The epicerie and campground, mentioned in other guides, have now closed. There is a bus service to St-Gaudens.

FACILITIES FOR STAGE 28

Fos

Gîte d'étape de Fos, at the time of writing it was uncertain if this basic place was still open.

Hôtel la Gentilhommière sells a few supplies, enough for a day/night, and offers the only reliable accommodation: tel 09 75 91 34 66. The owners can also advise on places to pitch a tent actually within the village.

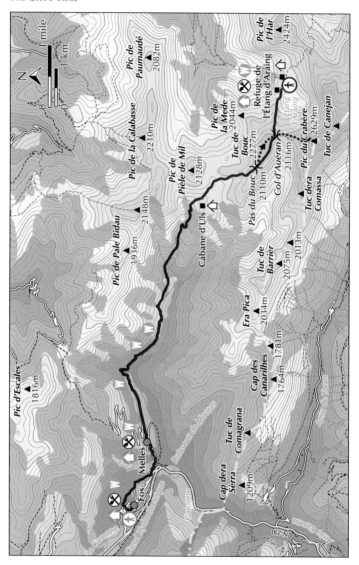

STAGE 29
Fos to Refuge de l'Étang d'Araing

Start	Fos
Distance	18km
Total ascent	1700m
Total descent	300m
Time	6hr 25min
High point	Col d'Auéran (2176m)

This long stage starts with a long road walk before a long climb up into wonderfully remote country for an easy crossing of the Col d'Auéran.

Veer right from the gîte d'étape and follow the waymarks which lead to a track at the edge of the village. Keep a close eye on the waymarks as you follow tracks and a minor road before returning to the main road (20min). Veer left up the D44H road, signed to Melles, passing the Cascade du Sériail and following signed and waymarked shortcuts to arrive at the Auberge de Crabère in **Melles** (45min). ▶

Note the exotic fish in the waterpoint at the auberge.

Continue through the hamlet and up the D44H, passing two picnic tables and several waterpoints and crossing a couple of streams before arriving at what appears to be the roadhead with a waterpoint (1hr 50min).

Despite being so high in the mountains, the **hoopoe** has been spotted here. It is unmistakeable with its long curved bill and pinkish plumage with striking black-and-white barred wings, tail and crest.

The small tarmac road continues a little further to a car park. Fork left up a concrete track to the final farm at Labach (2hr 10min). There is likely to be plenty of water on the ascent. If you want to camp, do so soon, as the first camping on the climb is in the vicinity of the Cabane d'Uls. Follow the path, crossing the main stream where a refreshing shower is possible in the waterfall (3hr 25min). Leave the wood (3hr 55min) and continue to climb steeply until the gradient eases as you reach a stream (4hr 35min). Climb more gently to reach a flat marshy area. The **Cabane d'Uls** is a bothy on a knoll about 200m on the right.

> This bothy isn't in the best of condition but is a useful stand-by in an emergency. The surrounding area provides good sheltered campsites and there are frequent camping opportunities ahead, until the final descent to Eylie in Stage 30.

Continue climbing on a clear path through pasture, passing well left of a shepherd's cabin and extensive mine workings to reach a shallow saddle, **Pas du Bouc** (5hr 45min, 2170m).

It would be easy to head E over Tuc de Bouc (2277m) and return to the GR10 by the SE ridge. The GR10

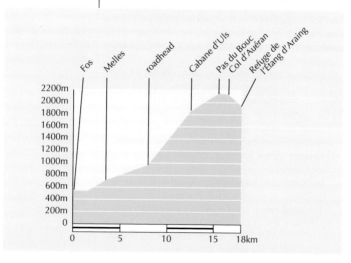

Refuge de l'Étang d'Araing

contours the SW slopes of Tuc de Bouc to reach **Col d'Auéran** (6hr, 2176m). A good path leads up the ridge to the S to the Pic de Crabère (2629m) (up and down in 90min).

The GR10 climbs slightly left before veering right and descending the grassy ridge to the **Refuge de l'Étang d'Araing** (6hr 25min, 1950m), with full refuge facilities and a waterpoint. ▸ It is possible to swim from the rocky shore of the reservoir.

The Pic de la Mede can look magical as it peeps out of mist, which frequently fills the valley to the N.

FACILITIES FOR STAGE 29

Melles

Auberge de Crabère, gîte d'étape, chambres d'hôtes accommodation and bar-restaurant: tel 06 15 09 04 58

Étang d'Araing

Refuge de l'Étang d'Araing (open June to mid October): tel 05 61 96 73 73, www.refuge-araing.fr

STAGE 30

Refuge de l'Étang d'Araing to Eylie-d'en-Haut

Start	Refuge de l'Étang d'Araing
Distance	8km
Total ascent	300m
Total descent	1300m
Time	3hr 5min
High point	Serre d'Araing (2221m)

This short stage starts with a quick climb to cross the Serre d'Araing before the descent to Eylie where you will pass many reminders of the mining industry which used to dominate the valley.

Continue down to the dam and follow the path below it. Keep straight on after crossing the original outlet stream to the corrie, pass a bothy and climb, always to the left of

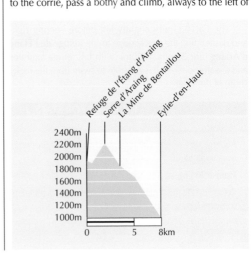

Cloud in the valley north from Serre d'Araing

the powerline, to the **Serre d'Araing** (1hr, 2221m) where there are the remains of the bucket lift of the old mine workings. ▸

The GR10 climbs right, about half way to the powerline, before descending grass slopes on the left. There are confusing strands to the path, but the route is either along or to the left of the powerline. A small stream (1hr 20min) provides the first water since the Étang d'Araing.

Pic de l'Har (2424m) to the left can be climbed, avoiding the obvious crags on the right (up and down in 50min).

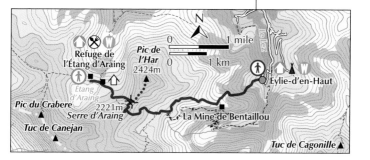

187

The two buildings on the right are used by a caving club and it is possible they will be able to find you somewhere to sleep, if anyone is in residence.

Be careful as the path finds its way through old mine workings before arriving at an old lead mine, **La Mine de Bentaillou** (1hr 35min, 1870m). ◄

The GR10 now veers left and contours along a path passing a number of mine entrances. After about 10min fork right and start the descent. The path is easy to follow but is rather slippery and unpleasant in places. After crossing the insignificant Col de la Catauère (1706m), the descent continues through more mining industry remains before the steep final descent through forest on a better path. Cross a woodland stream (2hr 45min) and finally arrive at a bridge across the stream at **Eylie-d'en-Haut**. The GR10 goes right to the gîte d'étape (3hr 5min, 990m) with a waterpoint outside.

The hamlet and picnic tables are left across the bridge. There is an aire de bivouac along the GR10, down by the river.

FACILITIES FOR STAGE 30

Gîte d'étape Eylie, Eylie-d'en-Haut: tel 05 61 96 14 00 or 06 75 59 22 96, www.giteseylie.jimdofree.com

STAGE 31

Eylie-d'en-Haut to Maison du Valier, Pla de la Lau

Start	Eylie-d'en-Haut
Distance	17km
Total ascent	1600m
Total descent	1700m
Time	8hr 10min
High point	Col de l'Arech (1802m), Col du Clot du Lac (1821m)

This long stage crosses two ridges with steep ascents and descents. There is a problem for those requiring accommodation, as this stage is too long for most walkers. Unless you are camping the solution is to stay at one of the five bothies on the route or to follow the alternative route via Bonac, which is described in Stages 31A and 32A, rejoining the GR10 at the Col de la Core in Stage 32.

A GR10 hiker climbing towards the Col d'Arech

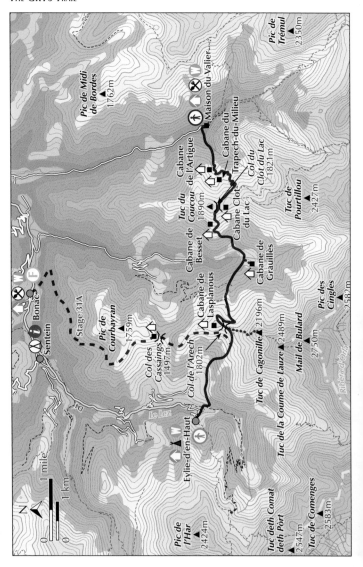

Continue E past the gîte d'étape, turning left (aire de bivouac on the right) to the bridge across **Le Lez** (960m).
Cross the river and turn right, then sharp left and follow a
good path, mainly through rough open country. Cross a
stream (50min) and soon enter a wood and climb steeply.
Once you are clear of the wood (1hr 55min), climb a
ridge covered in heather and bilberry. ▶ Eventually you
reach a path junction by an old stone cabin (2hr 25min,
1660m).

    ▶ The GR10 zigzags right, then left, crosses a stream
and follows a rising traverse to a signpost at the **Col de
l'Arech** (2hr 55min, 1802m).

    There is a sign indicating that **Mail de Bulard**
    (2750m) is three hours to the south. The interme-
    diate peak, Tuc de Cagonille (2196m), is easy (up
    and down in 80min) but Mail de Bulard looks more
    demanding.

Bilberry is a favourite
food for the bears that
live in the Ariège.

The GR10E goes
straight on here
as described in
Stage 31A.

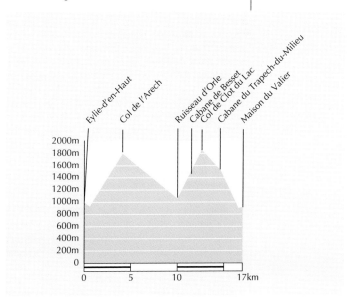

The GR10 goes left along the ridge, crosses a small col and veers right down the E ridge of Cap de l'Empaillou (1838m). There are exposed campsites near the Cabane de Lasplanous, which is just below the summit. This small bothy (space for only 3–4 people) is in decent condition. After a short descent the path veers right off the ridge and does a gently descending loop to reach the Cabane d'Arech from the S (3hr 20min, 1638m). ◄ Descend the cabin's access track to a sharp left bend and then keep straight on down a small path. Zigzag down the steep heather slope before turning right and contouring to cross a stream (3hr 50min). Descend easily through woods to a junction just before the Ruisseau d'Orle. The Cabane de Grauillès, a simple cabin in excellent condition, is 7min to the right.

The berger's dogs have been known to be very protective of their territory here! Give them a wide berth.

The GR10 crosses the stream on a bridge and veers left across pasture with poor campsites. Contour to the ruins of Flouquet (4hr 25min, 1081m) and continue across a stream, forking right immediately after another stream and starting to zigzag up the hill. Ignore a right turn for the Tour de Biros and immediately afterwards turn right and continue climbing. Leave the woods and arrive at the small **Cabane de Besset** (5hr 50min, 1540m). Camping is possible but the waterpoint in front of the cabin can be unreliable.

Climb easily up to the **Cabane Clot du Lac**, a small hut in great condition, at the Col de Clot du Lac (6hr 40min, 1821m). Exposed camping is possible but the waterpoint is likely to be dry.

Tuc du Coucou (1890m) to the left is a fine viewpoint (there and back in 12 minutes).

After dropping down a short distance, the GR10 goes right and climbs a little before starting a meandering descent down through pasture. Turn shap left at a (broken) signpost and zigzag down to the **Cabane du Trapech-du-Milieu**, with a waterpoint (7hr 15min, 1540m), which is sometimes occupied by shepherds and is not always available to hikers. Continue past **Cabane** de l'Artigue, another small bothy with a waterpoint and the last camping before the steep zigzagging descent through the woods to the road in the valley. Turn right past toilets and car parking. The GR10 goes left immediately after the toilets and follows the riverbank upstream to the **Maison du Valier** (8hr 10min, 927m) in the meadows of Pla de la Lau.

FACILITIES FOR STAGE 31

Gîte d'étape-auberge la Maison du Valier, gîte d'étape, chambres d'hôtes, a full meals service and picnic lunches: tel 05 61 01 01 01, www.maison-valier.fr

STAGE 31A
Eylie-d'en-Haut to Bonac

Start	Eylie-d'en-Haut
Distance	15km
Total ascent	700m
Total descent	1000m
Time	5hr 40min
High point	Below Col de l'Arech (1660m)

This easy, lower-level alternative along the GR10E is intended for those requiring accommodation or resupply and is continued in Stage 32A. It might also be considered as a bad weather option.

▶ Follow the GR10 as far as the junction by the old stone cabin (2hr 25min, 1660m) below the **Col de l'Arech**, as described in Stage 31. The GR10E follows a small but clear path which crosses a stream and passes just above some old mine buildings and traverses to the **Col des Cassaings** (3hr 20min, 1497m) with a powerline, campsites and a small bothy.

For route map, see Stage 31.

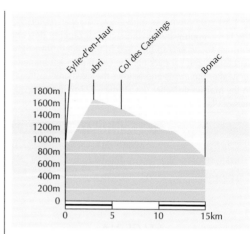

Continue contouring, veering right across a ridge (4hr). Don't miss an unexpected but waymarked right turn up a nebulous path (4hr 40min). This path becomes clearer and eventually zigzags before veering right down an old walled path (5hr 25min). Go straight across a track, which takes you to an aire de camping-car with a waterpoint and picnic tables. Cross the bridge into **Bonac** and keep straight on to Relais Montagnard, which is behind the church (5hr 40min, 706m). Sentein, with tourist office and campground, is 1.5km W of Bonac.

FACILITIES FOR STAGE 31A

Bonac

Relais Montagnard, gîte d'étape, chambres d'hôtes accommodation and bar-restaurant: tel 09 51 26 79 55

Sentein

Camping Municipal La Grange (open July and August): tel 05 61 96 18 74

STAGE 32

Maison du Valier, Pla de la Lau to Esbintz

Start	Maison du Valier
Distance	18km
Total ascent	1200m
Total descent	1300m
Time	7hr 10min
High point	Cap de Lauses ridge (1892m), N ridge of Pic de Crabère (1925m), N ridge Col d'Auédole (1730m)

This is another long, tough stage that will be best appreciated in good weather. There is an alternative route from Col de la Core – walkers who are intending to follow the main line of the GR10 to Couflens, as described in Stages 33 and 34, and who don't need accommodation or resupply, may prefer to take the high-level shortcut to Estours as described in Stage 32B.

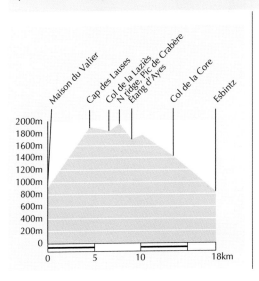

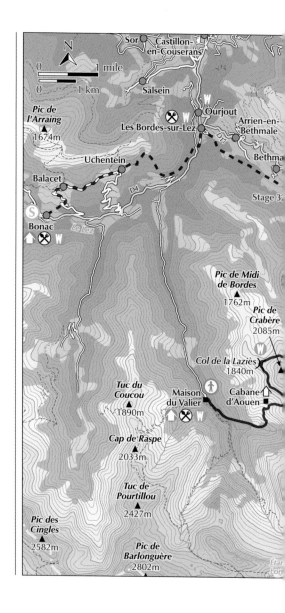

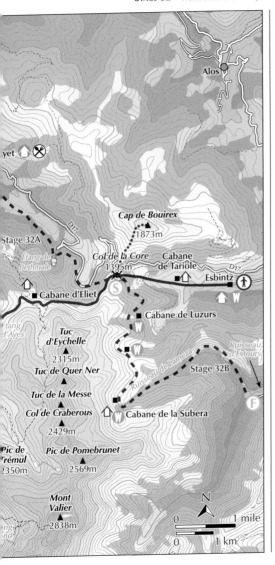

197

Sunrise from Col de la Core

Continue upstream, cross three bridges (waterpoint by first bridge) and follow the path up the left-hand bank of the Ruisseau du Ribérot. The path edges away from the river before reaching a junction with signpost. Turn left and climb into the Muscadet Valley and zigzag up to the left of the cascading stream. Cross the Ruisseau d'Aouen (55min) and continue climbing. The path veers left, leaves the forest and recrosses the Ruisseau d'Aouen (2hr 5min). The **Cabane d'Aouen** is about 100m to the left. This small hut offers a simple place to sleep if needed. Camping is possible, but far from ideal.

A fairly faint path zigzags E through wildflower meadows to the left of the stream to reach a junction just before reaching the Cap des Lauses ridge (3hr 5min, 1892m). Turn left and contour. There are good but exposed campsites where the path crosses two rocky ridges. Descend a little then climb to the **Col de la Laziès** (3hr 45min, 1840m). Cross and descend a short distance on a meandering path, passing a waterpoint, then fork right to a col on the N ridge of **Pic de Crabère** (4hr 10min, 1925m). ◄

Cross the col and descend to the N end of the **Étang d'Ayes** (4hr 30min, 1694m), a classic corrie lake with

Chamois (known as izard in the French Pyrenees) have been seen here. They seem to be much rarer on the GR10 than on the GR11 on the Spanish side of the Pyrenees.

the first good sheltered campsites on this stage. ▶ Cross the outlet stream on stepping stones and traverse roughly NE, ignoring any descending paths, to reach the Col d'Auédole (4hr 50min, 1730m). The GR10D, a variation not featured in this guide, descends E and soon passes the **Cabane d'Eliet**. There are better campsites ahead.

Turn right and follow the middle of three paths. When you reach good campsites (5hr 5min) veer left and descend to pass below crags and cross a stream, which is not always flowing. Traverse the woods to reach the Crête de Balame and descend this easy ridge to the **Col de la Core** (6hr, 1395m).

> The road pass, the Col de la Core, is a **meeting point** of variations on the GR10. The alternative route via Bonac, as described in Stages 31A and 32A, rejoins the GR10 here. It is also the start of a shortcut to the Estours Valley as described in Stage 32B. Cap de Bouirex (1873m) to the northeast is an easy peak to climb (up and down in a little less than two hours). There is plenty of parking as well as picnic tables and an interesting variation on the table d'orientation.

The next section is one of the 'messy' pastoral paths where you have to keep an extra careful eye on the way-marking. Descend SE, signed Piste de l'Aube. Go straight across the zigzagging road and descend the valley to reach a dirt road. Turn right and then left down a grassy track. Pass the **Cabane de Tariole** (1179m), a large and pleasant stone building that's more an old house than a mere cabin. Fork right, ignoring 'tractor tracks' and eventually pick up an old path which traverses the N slopes of the valley. Cross some small streams before arriving at the **Gîte d'étape Esbintz** (7hr 10min, 850m), with a waterpoint.

Swimming is excellent in the pool at the outlet of the lake.

FACILITIES FOR STAGE 32

Gîte d'étape Esbintz, full meals service and camping is possible: tel 09 63 64 15 96, www.gite-ferme-esbintz.fr

STAGE 32A

Bonac to Esbintz

Start	Bonac
Distance	25km
Total ascent	1200m
Total descent	1100m
Time	7hr
High point	Col de la Core (1395m)

This is a low-level, mainly pastoral continuation of Stage 31A for those requiring accommodation. The stage follows the GR10E from Bonac to just before the Étang de Bethmale, then the GR10D to Col de la Core where it rejoins the main GR10 to Esbintz. It would be possible to extend this stage slightly to stay in Seix or at the Gîte d'étape d'Aunac in Stage 33.

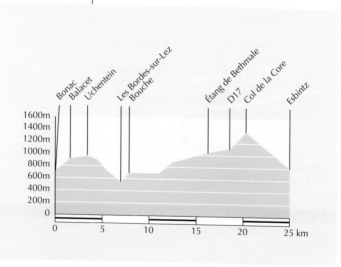

▶ From the Relais Montagnard, take the road heading N to the left of the shelter with a waterpoint. Take the path left of the last house, veer right then fork left and climb steeply. You may need to cross the fence on the right and go parallel to the path before regaining it higher up. Turn right at a junction with a grassy track and then fork left along the D704 road. Follow the D704 through **Balacet** (909m) and on to **Uchentein** (1hr 5min, 950m). After a switchback in the road, turn left along a track in the lower part of the hamlet, soon passing a waterpoint. Fork right along a path and start the descent. Go straight across a tarmac farm road, then turn left along the **D4** road, cross the bridge and follow the D4 into **Les Bordes-sur-Lez** (1hr 55min) where you will find waterpoints. ▶

The GR10 turns right immediately after a stream and heads SE out of the hamlet. It now follows the S slopes of the Vallée de Bathmale to the Étang de Bethmale. Turn right along a path by a waterpoint, cross the stream, fork left and climb steeply to a track with a buried pipeline. Turn left to Bouche (2hr 25min). Go straight across the

For route map, see Stage 32.

Go straight on if you need the restaurant or the public toilets, which are across the river in Ourjout.

Aqueduct in the Vallée de Bethmale

road and contour. After crossing a woodland stream, go right and left at a track, cross a small ridge and descend before resuming contouring along the pipeline, which surfaces as a small canal (aqueduct) in places.

At some farm buildings (3hr 15min) there is a sign left for le Petit Refuge in **Ayet**, across the valley. The GR10 now leaves the canal, veers right, crosses a stream and then zigzags up the hill before turning sharp right at a junction on a ridge. The waymarking is a little vague as you veer right of two farm buildings, then left of a third and follow an old walled path. Cross three small streams and follow a track to reach the road near the Étang de Bethmale. Turn left to cross the dam (4hr 30min, 1060m). There are toilets and a waterpoint in the car park. The ONF Refuge at the lake is only open to groups who book in advance.

The GR10E joins the GR10D and follows the left-hand of the two paths on the right, passing picnic tables to reach the **Étang de Bethmale**. If you're lucky enough to be here in October then you're in for a treat as the woodlands surrounding the lake put on one of the best autumnal light shows in the Pyrenees. Turn left immediately before the cabin with a waterpoint. After an initial steep climb, the path rises gently as it traverses above the road and descends slightly after crossing a stream to reach the **D17** road. Turn right and follow the D17 for 10min before turning sharp right and switchbacking up steep slopes to rejoin the GR10 at the **Col de la Core** (5hr 45min, 1395m). Continue as detailed in Stage 32 to the **Gîte d'étape Esbintz** (7hr, 850m).

FACILITIES FOR STAGE 32A

Le Petit Refuge, Ayet, small chambres d'hôtes providing evening meals: tel 06 31 32 96 42, www.lepetitrefuge.com

STAGE 32B

Col de la Core to Estours Valley

Start	Col de la Core
Distance	12km
Total ascent	300m
Total descent	1000m
Time	3hr 35min
High point	Col de Soularil (1579m)

This is a scenic higher-level shortcut from Col de la Core (in Stages 32 and 32A) to the Estours valley (in Stage 33) for those not requiring accommodation or resupply. There are frequent camping opportunities.

▸ Head right, down the road, then keep straight on at the first switchback, up the right-hand track. The track becomes a path, which generally contours. Fork right and

For route map, see Stage 32.

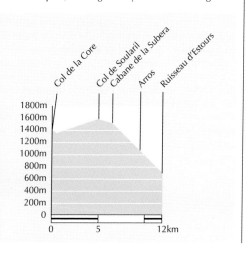

climb to pass above the **Cabane de Luzurs**, which has a waterpoint and sells cheese. The path contours again to reach the Cabane de Casabède. The cabin is closed to hikers but there is a waterpoint (1hr 20min, 1585m). Veer left and contour to the Col de Soularil (1579m). Cross the ridge and follow the path slightly right, S, veering right round the Crêtes des Hommes Morts. Cross a side stream before reaching the Ruisseau de Lameza, the outlet stream from the corrie (1hr 55min, 1500m). The **Cabane de la Subera**, which is in excellent condition and is well-equipped and comfortable, is in the corrie to the right.

> The berger (shephard) of the Cabane de la Subera welcomes walkers and has a room set aside as a bothy. There is also a waterpoint.

Cross the stream and descend on a path which is not always clear but stays well to the right of the stream. A short distance after the Cabane de Lameza veer left into the woods and veer further left to approach the stream. Descend above the right-hand side of the stream. The path is a little faint in places but it is important that you follow it as this is not a forest in which to lose the path. Don't be afraid to get your feet wet at a nasty little stream crossing on slippery rocks below a waterfall. Eventually you will arrive at meadows beside the stream with excellent campsites (2hr 55min). Continue down to a bridge, cross and descend to the left of the stream. Pass a cabin, reach a track beside the stream and follow this left for the final steep descent to the Ruisseau d'Estours by a hydro-electric power station. Cross the stream to rejoin the GR10 at the roadhead of the Estours valley (3hr 35min, 675m).

STAGE 33

Esbintz to Refuge d'Aula

Start	Esbintz
Distance	19km
Total ascent	1200m
Total descent	500m
Time	6hr 5min
High point	Col d'Oule (749m), Refuge d'Aula (1550m)

In good weather Stages 33 and 34, with the views of Mont Valier, will be the highlight of the Ariège. Unfortunately there is no accommodation on the GR10 between Aunac (or Seix) early on in Stage 33 and Rouze at the end of Stage 34. This distance is too far for the average hiker and the only option is to camp, stay in a bothy or follow the GRP Tour du Val du Garbet from Pont du Salat to St-Lizier as described in Stage 33A.

If you need to buy provisions divert to Seix early on in the stage. Once resupplied you can head south to rejoin the GR10 at Pont du Salat.

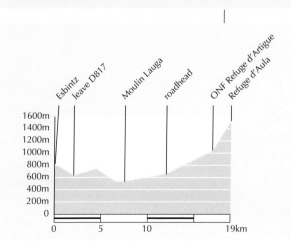

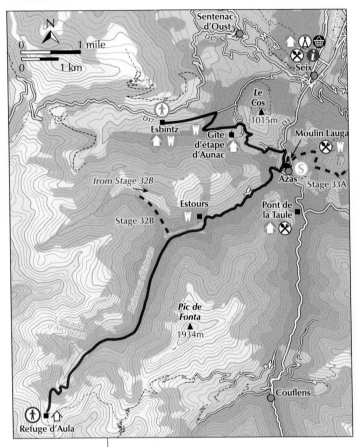

For Seix (4km) continue down the D817 turning right along the D37. From Seix, head south along the D3 to regain the GR10 at Pont du Salat (2km).

The GR10 veers right of the farm and follows the D817 road for about 2km to Borde de Galy (25min, 655m). ◄ The GR10 zigzags right down a track, passes a plastic barn with a waterpoint, crosses the stream and then veers left along a small path. This climbs to a better path, which contours before rising gently. Go straight on up a track, turn right along the road and then sharp left at a road junction (1hr) at a le Chemin de la Liberté monument. Turn right for the Gîte d'étape d'Aunac, which is not in the hamlet of Aunac.

The GR10 soon forks right up a good track and crosses the Col d'Oule (749m). Follow the main track, ignoring side turns as you zigzag down to reach the road below Esteyches. Turn right along the road and cross the Pont du Salat (550m) to reach the **D3**. ▶ Swimming is possible in the big pool under the bridge. Turn right, pass a canoe centre and arrive at **Moulin Lauga** (1hr 45min, 541m).

This is where the road from Seix rejoins the GR10.

At Moulin Lauga is a crêperie, picnic table and waterpoint. The Auberge des Deux Rivières is at Pont de la Taule about 1.5km to the SE.

Ruisseau d'Estours

This is where the shortcut (Stage 32B) from the Col de la Core rejoins the GR10 from the right.

Turn right up a minor road. Pass a waterpoint (2hr 30min) as you pass below **Estours**. Cross a bridge and continue up the track along the left-hand side of the **Ruisseau d'Estours** to another bridge (2hr 40min, 675m) at the roadhead. ◄

The GR10 continues up the left-hand side of the river, ignoring two left turns. Fork left shortly after the track becomes a path. Pass a cabin where camping should be possible in the meadow (3hr 20min).

Cross a side stream below a waterfall (can dry out in summer), pass a cabin and cross another stream below a more dramatic waterfall (4hr). Continue up to the now-closed ONF Refuge d'Artigue (4hr 30min, 1053m), with excellent campsites in a magnificent setting.

The path continues up the left-hand side of the open valley before zigzagging up into the woods. Cross bridges over two tumbling streams and cross a third stream to arrive at a large grassy corrie. Continue up the right-hand side of the corrie to the **Refuge d'Aula** (6hr 5min, 1550m).

This bothy has been totally renovated and is in excellent condition with beds for 12. You can get water from nearby small streams. There are excellent campsites in the corrie.

FACILITIES FOR STAGE 33

Seix

Seix is a large village with a tourist office, small supermarket and a selection of small shops and bar-restaurants, a campground and two hotels.

Tourist office: tel 05 61 96 00 01, www.haut-couserans.com

Auberge du Haut Salat: tel 05 61 66 88 03, www.aubergeduhautsalat.com

Auberge du Mont Valier: tel 05 61 04 79 24, www.maison-valier.fr

Camping le Haut-Salat: tel 05 61 66 81 78, www.camping-haut-salat.com

Aunac

Gîte d'étape d'Aunac, very plush place to rest up. Offers meals and picnic lunches: tel 06 48 90 78 59, www.domaine-aunac.fr

Pont de la Taule

Auberge des Deux Rivières: tel 05 61 66 83 57, www.auberge-des-deux-rivieres.fr

STAGE 33A

*Esbintz to Saint-Lizier-d'Ustou using
the Tour du Val du Garbet*

Start	Esbintz
Distance	20km
Total ascent	800m
Total descent	900m
Time	6hr 30min
High point	S slopes, Serre de la Plagne (1120m)

Stage 33A includes a short section, from Azas to Le Trein, of the multi-day circular Tour du Val du Garbet. It bypasses Stages 33, 34 and 35 and is included for those requiring manned accommodation as the GR10 from Esbintz, Seix or Aunac to Rouze is too far for most hikers. The route is easy to follow with red/yellow waymarks. There is camping about half way but only a few streams of dubious quality, which are unlikely to withstand a drought. You will be traversing the steep south slopes of Serre de la Plagne on paths of packed mud, which will be very slippery in the wet. It is strongly recommended that you use walking poles for security.

Follow Stage 33 to the canoe centre just N of **Moulin Lauga** (1hr 35min). Turn left up a minor road, signed to Azas. After two switchbacks fork left and keep straight on into Azas (640m). Switchback left in the middle of the hamlet, signed to Mirabat, and climb, ignoring any contouring paths, to a junction signed Bois du Mirabat (2hr 25min, 810m). Keep straight on climbing to a high

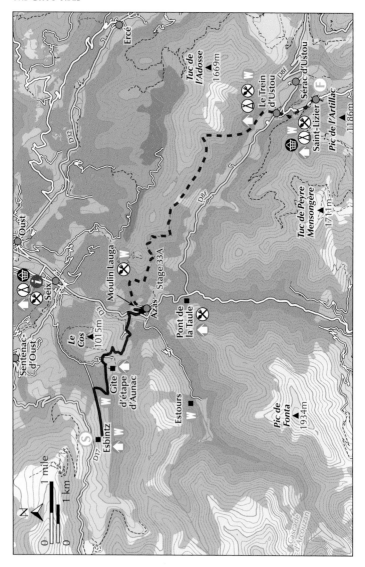

Traversing the steep slopes on the Tour du Val du Garbet

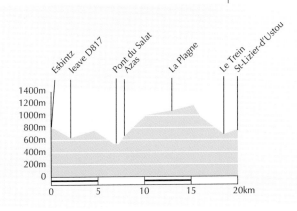

point on the S ridge of Mirabet (3hr 10min) and descend slightly to reach an old barn. Climb again to reach a barn in a meadow with good campsites (4hr 10min).

Contour along a path, which becomes very rocky for a while. Cross a woodland stream (5hr 10min) and zig-zag steeply down before resuming the traverse to reach a signpost for Fontaine du Gouilly. There is no waterpoint here! Continue the descent, carefully following the way-marks to cross the Alet river by Camping le Montagnou in Le Trein-d'Ustou. Turn left along the riverbank to arrive at the centre of **Le Trein-d'Ustou** (6hr 10min, 675m). Turn left and then right past a waterpoint on the corner. Climb a tarmac track past the Château du Trein-d'Ustou and along the D38 road to rejoin the GR10 on the outskirts of **Saint-Lizier-d'Ustou** (6hr 30min, 740m). Follow directions in Stage 36 for the continuation of the hike.

FACILITIES FOR STAGE 33A

Le Trein-d'Ustou

Camping le Montagnou: tel 05 61 66 94 97, www.lemontagnou.com

See Stage 35 for facilities in **Saint-Lizier-d'Ustou**.

STAGE 34

Refuge d'Aula to Rouze

Start	Refuge d'Aula
Distance	16km
Total ascent	700m
Total descent	1300m
Time	4hr 30min
High point	Bouche d'Aula (1998m)

The easy crossing of the Bouche d'Aula gives magnificent views back to Mont Valier (2838m).

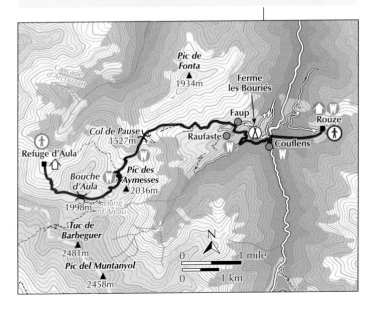

Mont Valier from above the Refuge d'Aula

Red blackstarts are often spotted in this area.

Pic des Aymesses (2036m) to the E of the lake is an easy summit from here.

In bad weather you may prefer to follow the road.

The GR10 zigzags up the grassy slopes on the back left of the corrie to arrive at a false col (1hr 5min). Here you will find good campsites with magnificent views NW to Mont Valier. ◄ Continue easily up to the **Bouche d'Aula** (1hr 20min, 1998m). Contour left of the large sinkhole, cross a small col and contour right before descending to the Refuge ONF d'Areau at the rather dirty-looking **Étang d'Areau** (1888m). As with other ONF refuges this is only available to groups booking in advance. ◄

Turn left down the dirt road, which is 'followed' all the way to Faup with numerous shortcuts of the switchbacks. ◄ Soon, shortcut right and cross the road at the first meeting. Pass a waterpoint just before returning to the road. The next shortcut is on the left after which you pass the Cabane d'Areau and again shortcut left. Cross a stream and then turn left along the road. Pass a small pipe fed by springwater in a crag to the right of the road and continue to the car park at a col with a sign saying it is the Col de Pause (2hr 15min, 1527m).

Contour left from immediately below the car park to reach the actual **Col de Pause** and switch back right, back to the road. The next shortcut is left after a switchback in the road and then keep straight on at another switchback. When you next meet the road it is tarmacked and you follow it until you switch back left after a right switchback in the road (3hr). Pass a waterpoint and descend through the small hamlet of **Faup**, then descend its access road, turning left then right at a junction before switching back left down a path immediately before Raufaste. You soon start zigzagging steeply through the woods to the basic campground at the **Ferme les Bouriés** (3hr 25min, 807m).

Cross the stream and turn left down the road to **Couflens**. Turn left through the hamlet (3hr 40min, 702m). There is a waterpoint with toilets and a picnic table and there is a bus service between Couflens and Seix. Cross the Salat river, ignore a second bridge and then turn right through a gate in front of the last house before the road forks. Climb steeply up the path to the left of the stream. Cross and recross the stream and pass a waterpoint as you arrive at the **Gîte d'étape de Rouze** (4hr 30min, 930m)

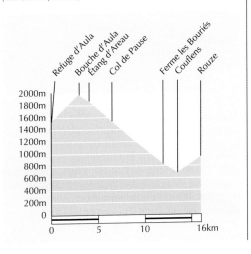

215

FACILITIES FOR STAGE 34

Camping Ferme les Bouriés: tel 0561 048 584,
www.fermelesbouries.jimdofree.com

Rouze

Gîte d'étape de Rouze, meals and small shop providing basic provisions for picnic lunches: tel 04 68 20 40 39, www.ferme-de-rouze.fr

STAGE 35

Rouze to Saint-Lizier-d'Ustou

Start	Rouze
Distance	7km
Total ascent	600m
Total descent	800m
Time	3hr
High point	Col de la Serre du Cot (1546m)

A strong walker could combine this short stage with Stage 34. In good weather you might like to climb Pic de la Tese (2255m) from Col de la Serre du Cot.

Climb steeply from just below the gîte d'étape, then turn sharp right. Start zigzagging up the hill. Careful attention to the waymarking is required as there are many side turns to ignore. Pass through a farm, cross a woodland stream (45min) and eventually exit the woods to arrive at the grassy **Col de la Serre du Cot** (1hr 40min, 1546m) with magnificent views to E and W and with good exposed campsites. There is a waterpoint about 5min contouring ENE from the col, but it shouldn't be relied upon, and a small cabin about 5min along the ridge to the S which could be used as a bothy.

Gîte d'étape de Rouze

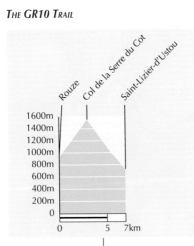

From the col **Tuc de Peyre Mensongère** (1711m) to the left is an easy climb but not really worth the effort (up and down in 35 minutes). Of more interest is the easy ridge to the south over Peak 1797 and on to the **Pic de la Tèse** (2255m) from where there are fine views of the frontier ridge (a return journey will take just under three hours). It is easiest to bypass the first two knolls on the left and then three minor tops on the right.

From the col, descend left and go straight across a track and zigzag down a good path through the woods. Go straight across a track (2hr 20min), cross a small woodland stream and pass many ruined farm buildings before reaching a good track. If you are wanting to camp before Saint-Lizier, you should do so here.

The alternative route, 33A (Tour du Val du Garbet), rejoins the GR10 here.

Follow the track across the Ruisseau de Bielle (790m) and down to the D38 road. ◄ Turn right into **Saint-Lizier-d'Ustou** (3hr, 740m).

The gîte d'étape is on the left, then there is a waterpoint and further down a campground, a swimming pool, a shop which sells original camping gas, and toilets opposite the bar-restaurant. There is a bus service from Saint-Lizier to Seix.

FACILITIES FOR STAGE 35

Saint-Lizier-d'Ustou

Gîte d'étape la Colline Verte, gîte d'étape, chambres d'hôtes and provides meals: tel 05 61 04 68 17, www.gite-colline-verte.com

Camping Municipal: tel 06 88 85 94 47, www.ustou-camping-municipal.com

Alternative accommodation at Bidous is detailed in Stage 36.

STAGE 36

Saint-Lizier-d'Ustou to Aulus-les-Bains

Start	Saint-Lizier-d'Ustou
Distance	23km
Total ascent	1400m
Total descent	1400m
Time	9hr 5min; shortcut from Jasse du Fouillet 6hr
High point	Col d'Escots (1618m), NE ridge, Pic de Mont Rouge (1600m)

This stage is too long for most walkers but it can be shortened by a direct descent to Aulus-les-Bains from Jasse du Fouillet. After taking the shortcut you could take a 'rest day' to explore the spectacular Val d'Ars. The alternative route via Bidous is only likely to be used by walkers who prefer to stay at Bidous than Saint-Lizier.

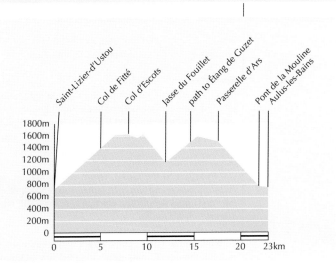

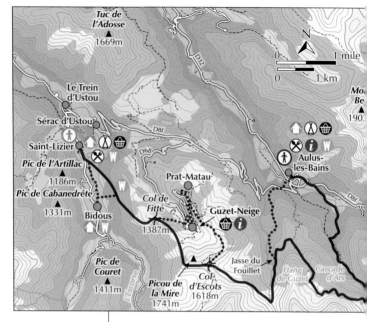

Head S out of Saint-Lizier and turn left across a footbridge at the end of the village. Turn right to a junction.

Alternative route via Bidous
If you require the Gîte d'étape l'Escolan, go right at the junction and continue parallel to the river, ignoring lots of turns, to a junction signed Marees du Pouech (15min). The left turn is the path to return to the GR10, but keep straight on to reach Bidous. Gîte d'étape l'Escolan is across the bridge (20min).

To rejoin to the GR10, return to the Marees du Pouech junction and turn right. Ignore a switchback 5min later and climb steeply to a junction with the GR10 (1hr 10min).

Fork left for the GR10, cross a track and climb steeply through the woods, passing a spring-fed pipe (45min).

In a dry summer, assuming it is running, this could be your last water for 3hr. Reach a path junction (1hr 5min, 1000m). ▶ Continue climbing, with occasional switchbacks, to arrive at the **Col de Fitté** (2hr, 1387m).

This is where the alternative route rejoins from the right.

> This broad grassy col has good campsites and there are also plenty of camping opportunities ahead. Another option is to leave the GR10 on the track that contours E to the ski resort of Guzet-Neige (20min). In Guzet-Neige a shop and the tourist information office are open in July and August. There is also the option to continue up the D68 to Prat-Matau with a better shop, bar-restaurant and swimming pool, also open in July and August (45min). To return to the GR10, follow the road to the bar-restaurant at the Col d'Escots to rejoin the GR10 (1hr 25min from the Col de Fitté).

The GR10 climbs the ridge to the right of the col. You should follow the GR10, which is to the right and is steep and slippery in places rather than the better path up the centre of the ridge. This is a cycle path where mountain bikes descend at high speed and not necessarily under full control! Eventually (2hr 50min) the GR10 forks right and contours round the SW ridge of **Picou de la Mire** (1741m) to arrive at the **Col d'Escots** (3hr 15min, 1618m). Turn right along the track and follow it to the right of the Chalet de Beauregard, which is a bar-restaurant (open 10.00am–11.00pm in July and August).

Veer left as the track veers right for an up and down traverse of the steep N slopes of Pic de Freychet. Cross a small stream (3hr 45min) and a bigger one shortly afterwards before descending a little to reach the Ruisseau de Fouillet where there are campsites in a hanging valley (4hr 5min).

Cross the bridge and turn left down a rough rocky path. You will soon be high above the cascading stream and dramatic waterfalls of the Ruisseau de Fouillet. Continue to a path junction signed Jasse du Fouillet (4hr 50min, 1170m).

Shortcut to Aulus-les-Bains

For the alternative direct route to Aulus-les-Bains along the Tour du Val du Garbet, keep straight on following red/yellow waymarks. Pass a cabin in a clearing where camping is possible with water nearby, cross a small stream and fork left. After a further left fork continue descending to the **D8F** road. Go straight across, keep straight on at a gate and turn left down the road to reach the tourist office in **Aulus-les-Bains** (6hr).

From Jasse du Fouillet, turn right for the GR10 and climb to cross the N ridge of Pic du Mont Rouge (1600m) at the Plateau de Souliou. There are campsites as you cross the ridge. Turn right after crossing a small, possibly dry stream, continue climbing to cross the outlet stream

Le Garbet on the approach to Aulus-les-Bains

from the **Étang de Guzet** and on to a path junction (5hr 50min). ▸ The GR10 continues to climb and emerges from the woods to reach a boggy grassy pass. There follows a rough, undulating rocky traverse along the steep N slopes of Cap du Pis Blanc. Cross several streams before reaching the Ruisseau d'Ars at the Passerelle d'Ars where camping is possible (7hr 5min, 1485m).

Fork right if you want to visit the lake, where camping and swimming is possible.

Cross the bridge, turn left and descend a tough rocky path. ▸ Eventually cross the stream on a bridge (8hr 10min) and the going eases as you join a track. About 10min later, turn right down a path and descend steeply back to the stream. There are possible campsites as you follow the Ruisseau d'Ars stream down before crossing Le Garbet river at the Pont de la Mouline. Continue along a grassy track to a junction (8hr 50min, 780m).

You will have to explore short paths to the left of the GR10 to get the best views of the spectacular waterfalls and cascades of the Ruisseau d'Ars.

The GR10 goes sharp right here but most hikers will keep straight on to reach the **D8** road to be followed left into **Aulus-les-Bains** (9hr 5min, 750m).

There are GR waymarks from the outskirts of the village to the Gîte d'étape le Presbytère, which is just downhill from the church. The other facilities, including a tourist office, shops, other accommodation, camping, bar-restaurants and the spa, Thermes du Aulus-les-Bains, are down the D8. There is a bus service to St-Girons via Seix.

FACILITIES FOR STAGE 36

Bidous

Gîte d'étape l'Escolan: tel 05 61 96 58 72, www.lescolan.com

Aulus-les-Bains

Tourist office: tel 05 61 96 02 22

Gîte d'étape le Presbytère, gîte d'étape, chambres d'hôtes accommodation and meals: tel 07 68 07 41 07, www.giteaulus.com

Gîte d'étape la Goulue: tel 05 61 66 53 01

Hôtel les Oussaillès: tel 05 61 96 03 68

Camping le Coulédous: tel 05 61 66 43 56, www.camping-aulus-couledous.com

STAGE 37

Aulus-les-Bains to Refuge des Étangs de Bassiès

Start	Aulus-les-Bains
Distance	11km
Total ascent	1200m
Total descent	300m
Time	5hr 5min
High point	Port de Bassiès (1933m)

After an easy ascent to the Port de Saleix, this next stage brings a tougher crossing of the Port de Bassiès with spectacular granite scenery.

To return to the GR10, follow the D8 Col d'Agnès road to the right of the tourist office, passing a picnic site. When the road bends right at the edge of the village, fork right along the grassy track to reach the Pont de la Mouline

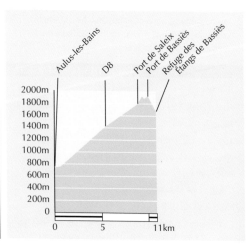

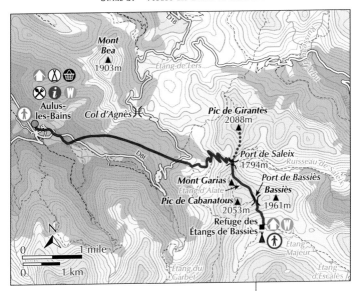

junction. Camping would be possible here or early on the climb. Fork left up an old walled path, then take a poorly waymarked left turn, which brings you back to the D8. Go straight across the road and follow a good path as it climbs easily. Fork left (45min) and cross a number of woodland streams, eventually returning to the **D8** (2hr 20min, 1400m). Camping is possible at regular intervals until you reach Étang d'Escalès in Stage 38. Go straight across the road, passing a picnic table, and cross the pasture of the Plateau de Coumebière.

Ten minutes later, fork left past a waterpoint, and begin climbing switchbacks. Fork left at an unmarked junction and continue climbing to reach the **Port de Saleix** (3hr 40min 1794m). There are good campsites just before you reach the col. ▶

There is an easy path up Pic de Girantès (2088m) to the left.

Now climb steeply right up the N ridge of **Mont Garias** (2006m). About halfway up fork left (a small path continues up to the summit) and descend slightly to pass **Étang d'Alate**. There are no obvious campsites,

An orri on the approach to the Refuge des Étangs de Bassiès

Pic de Cabanatous (2053m) to the W and Montagne de Bassiès (1961m) to the E.

but swimming is possible from the rocky shore. The path is rough and rocky in this scenic granite terrain. Climb gently SE to a shallow grassy col, the **Port de Bassiès** (4hr 30min, 1933m). ◄

Descend to reach a couple of orri (old stone shelters) at a path junction. The GR10 goes straight on but you will probably want to veer right to the **Refuge des Étangs de Bassiès** which is reached in 5min (5hr 5min, 1665m).

The Refuge des Étangs de Bassiès has full refuge facilities as well as an aire de bivouac and a small selection of provisions.

FACILITIES FOR STAGE 37

Bassiès

Refuge des Étangs de Bassiès (staffed mid May to late September): tel 06 89 40 65 00, www.refugedebassies.fr

STAGE 38

Refuge des Étangs de Bassiès to Marc

Start	Refuge des Étangs de Bassiès
Distance	11km
Total ascent	100m
Total descent	800m
Time	3hr 20min
High point	Refuge des Étangs de Bassiès (1665m)

This is a short downhill stage which should give you time to resupply at Auzat. The GR10 doesn't actually visit Auzat or Vicdessos, which have the only shops between Saint-Lizier and Bolquère, but it is possible to cut down to Auzat with various options for regaining the GR10 as detailed below and shown on the Stage 39 map. It would also be possible to resupply at Auzat by descending from Goulier at the end of Stage 39.

Return to the junction with the GR10 and turn right, passing left of several natural lakes and then two reservoirs: **Étang Majeur** (the easiest swimming is from the rocks across the dam) and **Étang d'Escalès** (swimming possible). A little below the dam, cross the outlet of the Étang d'Escalès on a precarious-looking but beautifully engineered stone bridge (1hr 10min, 1580m). If you want to camp before reaching the valley you should do so here. The GR10 now traverses the NE slopes of Pic de Sauve (2315m), crossing a couple of small streams and a spring-fed pipe (1hr 40min), which may

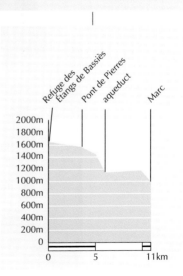

227

be the last water before Marc (but in a dry summer it can stop flowing) before turning steeply down to a junction on an old aqueduct (2hr 10min, 1160m).

To visit Auzat

It is possible to deviate from the GR10 to visit Auzat from Stages 38 or 39, but it is easiest to do so from here. Take the lower right turn if you want the direct route to Auzat. This excellent path goes straight across a hydro-electric road and forks left at a junction by a stream. Continue down to and cross a bridge over the Rivière de Vicdessos to reach the D108 (2hr 40min). Turn left and follow this road to **Auzat** (3hr 30min) passing the Auberge du Montcalm as you reach the village.

A disused aqueduct, Vicdessos Valley

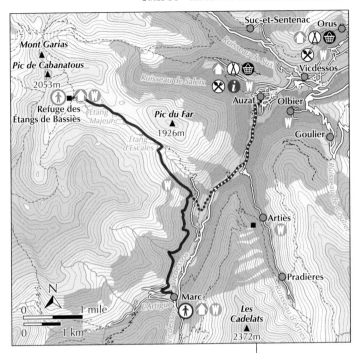

Auzat and Vicdessos (about 15min further on) are
villages with facilities for tourists. The tourist office
is at the E end of Auzat with a small store alongside. There is a small supermarket at the E end of
Vicdessos along with the best bar-restaurants. Both
villages have campgrounds.

There are five main options to return to the GR10
depending on how much of the GR10 you decide to cut.
There are several possibilities for reaching Marc or you
could miss out Marc altogether.

- Return to the GR10 at the old aqueduct.
- Head S from Auzat and fork right to rejoin the GR10
  at Marc (about 6km).

- Head S from Auzat and fork left to rejoin the GR10 at Artiès (about 4km).
- Head S from Auzat and after crossing the river, turn left (no sign). Turn right, signed to Goulier with infrequent yellow waymarks, and then left up an old path, which leads easily to **Olbier**. Turn right at the waterpoint and climb, ignoring a number of turns. Fork left and cross a stream to arrive at a waterpoint on the 'main' street of **Goulier**. The GR10 goes right and then left, under an arch, at another waterpoint.
- Follow the road from Vicdessos to Goulier. This is not recommended as it isn't a safe road for walkers. For more details see map for Stage 39.

The GR10 takes the upper right-hand turn and climbs very gently along the concrete top of a disused aqueduct. A stream is crossed, but there is no access to the water. Eventually go round a tower and veer right along the top of a pipe, reaching a minor road in about 150m (3hr). Turn left along the road to a road junction and fork left down a path and left again. Go straight across a road to a waterpoint. Go down the road, cross a bridge and turn left past the church to a junction with the D8 in **Marc** (3hr 20min, 1010m).

> There are toilets and a waterpoint by the junction. The holiday complex, Villages Vacances de Marc, which runs the Gîte d'étape de Marc, is a short distance S of the junction.

FACILITIES FOR STAGE 38

Auzat

Tourist office: tel 05 61 64 87 53

Auberge du Montcalm, mainly intended for groups using the new sports complex, but it welcomes GR10 hikers and offers full meals service: tel 05 61 05 89 25

Camping la Vernière: tel 05 61 64 84 46, www.laverniere.fr

Vicdessos

Camping la Bexanelle: tel 05 61 64 82 22, www.campingariege.eu

Marc

Gîte d'étape de Marc, offers meals and basic supplies for picnic lunches: tel 05 61 64 88 54, wwww.marc-montmija.com

See also Gîte d'étape de Mounicou, early in Stage 39.

STAGE 39

Marc to Goulier

Start	Marc
Distance	26km
Total ascent	1500m
Total descent	1400m
Time	9hr 10min; see stage description below for alternative route timings
High point	Refuge de Prunadière (1615m), above Étang d'Izourt (1780m)

This stage takes a circuitous route, crossing two ridges which head north from the watershed on the border with Andorra. There are three main options if you require manned accommodation and this very long stage is too long for you. Option 1: take the shortcut from Pradières saving about two hours (also a sensible option in bad weather). Option 2: descend to Auzat from Artiès. Option 3: break the stage by following GR10A to the Refuge de l'Étang Fourcat rejoining the GR10 above the Étang d'Izourt. This option is longer and tougher than the GR10, but it takes you into spectacular Alpine terrain. You still have a very long first day.

There are also two alternative options if you are camping and don't require the gîte d'étape at Goulier and don't need to resupply at Auzat. Either follow the GR10B which traverses to the Goulier-Neige ski area and continues to contour to rejoin the GR10 at the Col de l'Esquérus in Stage

40 (about 20 minutes shorter than the GR10). Alternatively, the spectacular good weather option (actually a little easier than the GR10) would be to traverse Pique d'Endron (2472m) and rejoin the GR10 at the Col de Grail in Stage 40 (about one hour longer than following the GR10B). Options for returning to the GR10 if you have visited Auzat are given in Stage 38.

Look out for the treecreeper in this forest. This little brown bird creeps around the vertical tree-trunks searching for hidden insects.

Continue up the road. Keep straight on along a path when the road switches back left, to reach another road (15min). Mounicou is across the river with the Café-gîte d'étape de Mounicou.

The GR10 continues along the road then turns left up a path signed to Artiès. Follow the waymarks carefully at a number of junctions then follow a good path which zigags up to the **Cabane de Prunadière** (1hr 55min, 1615m). ◄

This basic cabin has no beds in it but could serve as a night shelter. There's a waterpoint, which is the

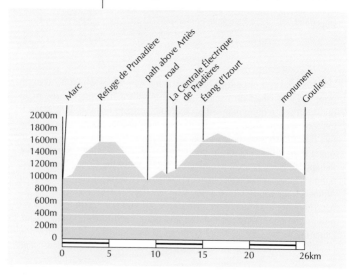

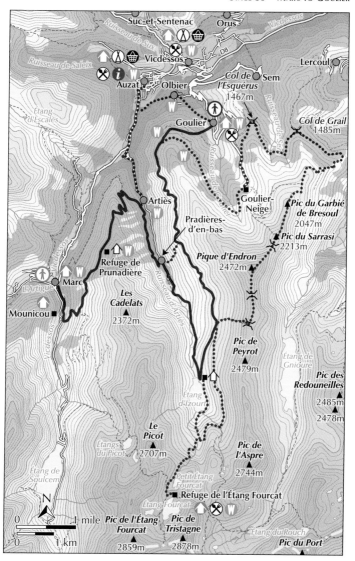

233

Miner's path in Artiès valley

last water before Artiès. There are no obvious camp-sites on the ascent, but a few possibilities for the imaginative camper.

Descend a little before resuming the traverse to reach the N ridge of **Les Cadelats** (2hr 15min), which has the best campsites between Marc and Artiès. Descend the ridge for a short distance before starting a gentle zigzag-ging descent. A more direct path from Marc joins from the left before you reach a junction just above **Artiès** (3hr 5min). ▸ The GR10 goes right and soon forks right as it climbs to a good path which climbs gently up the val-ley. Turn left (3hr 45min) and zigzag down, turn left past the remains of **Pradières-d'en-bas** and cross the stream to reach the road (3hr 50min). Turn right along the road. There are frequent water and camping opportunities as you climb to the Étang d'Izourt.

Turn left if you need the waterpoint or toilets in Artiès (985m) or wish to descend to Auzat.

Shortcut from Pradières-d'en-bas
A few minutes later, to follow a shorter variation of the GR10, go left by some houses. This variation climbs about 450m up the steep hillside to rejoin the GR10 at Coumasses-Grandes (1hr 40min from Pradières).

The GR10 continues up the road, passing a large car park and power station (1183m), la Centrale Électrique de Pradières. Pass the Orri de la Coume, three old stone huts. The higher one on the left could be used for an emergency bivouac. Continue up to the E end of the Barrage d'Izourt. There is a large room for hikers at the N end of the cabin on the left (5hr 45min, 1647m). Camping is possible.

Alternative route (GR10A) via Refuge de l'Étang Fourcat (stage total 12hr 5min)
▸ Follow the path above the E shore of the Étang d'Izourt. At the S end cross a stream below a waterfall, cross a second stream and climb the steep slope up to a small corrie occupied by the Orri de la Caudière (1hr

Times given below are from the Étang d'Izourt dam.

There are magnificent views over Étang Fourcat enclosed by the Pic de Malcaras, Pic de l'Étang Fourcat and Pic de Tristagne.

10min). Camping is possible. You will return to this junction on your way back from the refuge.

Turn right for the refuge, cross a bridge, if it hasn't been washed away, and follow a clear path up to a little col and a very tall cairn, Hommes de Pierre (2hr 25min, 2350m). Follow the path to the right of the **Petit Étang Fourcat**, with excellent campsites, and climb before veering left over roches moutonnées to the **Refuge de l'Étang Fourcat** (3hr, 2445m) with full refuge facilities. ◄

From the refuge, return to the Orri de la Caudière (4hr 15min) and turn right. Climb a little then start traversing. Cross a stream and an awkward section of rocky path using a handrail (5hr 10min). Pass a collection of orri, where camping is possible, and continue to the junction with the GR10 (5hr 50min). The junction is not signed and could be confusing. It is just before a lone tree and the GR10 comes up from back left.

The GR10 goes back sharp left from the cabin at the Barrage d'Izourt and follows a path, which is initially very faint. It becomes clearer and eventually crosses a water pipeline to reach a vague junction with the GR10A by a lone tree (6hr 20min, 1780m). In this section you cross a number of streams of dubious quality and longevity.

Alternative route traversing Pique d'Endron to Col de Grail (4hr 20min)

Fork right, following yellow waymarks, if you are going to traverse Pique d'Endron or if you want campsites, as after this camping opportunities are very limited. There is no water until the Col de Grail. You soon reach a flat area with good camping, as well as several orri, one of which is still used by the shepherd. Locate a faint path by the top right-hand orri and follow it as it switchbacks easily up to the ridge. Turn left along the ridge to the summit of **Pique d'Endron** (2472m).

Descend the NE ridge (Crête du Surrazi) via a few easy rocksteps. Keep straight on when the 'tourist route' drops down left to the Goulier-Neige ski centre. Eventually you will pick up a poor track, heading roughly NNE. Follow this track as it veers E and zigzags down, passing a cabin. Eventually the track veers W into the woods. Fork left and follow the track to the **Col de Grail**.

The GR10 forks left and starts a gentle descending traverse on an old path. The path is generally easy but it is very exposed and in places it has been chiselled out of the rockface and there are a few awkward rocksteps. Eventually the alternative direct route from Pradières joins from the left (7hr 20min). Here a cave has been converted into a shelter, Abri de Coumasses, which could be used for an emergency bivouac.

There is a monument on the knoll on the left commemorating the opening of the Ariège section of the GR10 on 10 October 1975.

The path now contours, enters the woods and eventually reaches a path junction (8hr 30min, 1410m). ▶

Alternative route via Goulier-Neige ski area (1hr 30min)
If you don't need the gîte d'étape at Goulier and are not intending to descend from Goulier to resupply in Auzat, it would be sensible to follow the GR10B from this junction. Fork right, cross a track and then fork left. Join a bigger track and pass the Fontaine de Brosquet which has reliable water (camping possible). Fork left at a turning circle. Cross a stream to reach a junction, fork right and climb, switchbacking right and left before arriving at the Goulier-Neige ski area (1hr 10min, 1500m). There are no facilities open in the summer apart from the waterpoint at the far end of the car park. Camping is possible, but you will have to search for 'cow-free' grass! Walk through the car park and follow the road for about 1km before forking right along a good track, then right along a path to reach the junction with the GR10 in Stage 40 (1hr 30min).

The GR10 forks left and passes the Refuge ONF de Bertasque. As with other ONF refuges this is only open to groups booking in advance, however, the waterpoint and picnic tables should be available to hikers. Continue straight across a track and turn right at the next

If you want to descend to Auzat you should follow the reverse of the route via Olbier described in Stage 38.

crossing of the track. Turn left down a steep path to arrive at Goulier (1110m). Go under the arch into the 'main' street, turn left and then, by a waterpoint, turn right under another arch to reach the Goulier 'bypass'. The GR10 goes straight across but you will probably want to turn left along the road for the gîte d'étape (9hr 10min). ◄

FACILITIES FOR STAGE 39

Mounicou

Café-gîte d'étape de Mounicou, no meals but you can get snacks at the café: tel 06 76 80 46 30

Refuge de l'Étang Fourcat (open late June to late September): tel 05 61 65 43 15 or or 06 18 20 08 20, www.refuge-fourcat.com

Goulier

Gîte d'étape Relais d'Endron, full meals service: tel 09 87 37 06 19, https://relaisdendron.traveleto.com/

STAGE 40

Goulier to Siguer

Start	Goulier
Distance	13km
Total ascent	500m
Total descent	800m
Time	3hr 5min
High point	Col de Lercoul (1549m)

This is an easy stage crossing a low pass. After a couple of days contouring on steep slopes, the GR10 returns to its 'rollercoaster' profile before coming to a halt for the day in tiny Siguer.

Return S along the road from the gîte d'étape to rejoin the GR10, turn left and climb to reach a track at the **Col de**

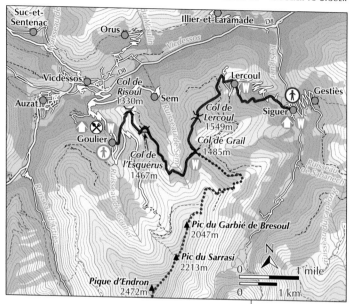

Risoul where camping is possible. Turn right and immediately fork left along a good path, which contours above
the track to reach a junction (50min). ▶ Switch back left
and climb to the **Col de l'Esquérus** (1hr, 1467m). From
here you contour, taking the contouring option at junctions and cross a stream before joining a good track
which crosses a bigger stream before reaching the **Col de
Grail** (1hr 30min, 1485m). ▶

> There is a reliable waterpoint 250m along the track
> to the right. Camping is possible.

Turn left up the track past the Refuge de Grail. This is
an ONF refuge for groups booking in advance. Fork right
up a path to reach the shallow **Col de Lercoul** (1hr 50min,
1549m). Cross the col and descend to a good track. Turn
left and a few minutes later, at a small clearing, turn right
and descend to a bigger clearing with picnic table and

The alternative
GR10B route
joins here.

The alternative route
which traverses Pique
d'Endron meets
the route here.

239

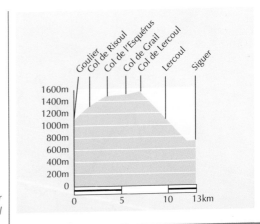

*Looking over Siguer
back towards Lercoul*

good camping. Turn right down the road and shortcut right then left to return to the road just above **Lercoul**. Turn left and right and descend to the main square with waterpoint (2hr 25min, 1120m).

Go down a cobbled alley to follow a path which approaches the road, then contours for a bit before forking left a couple of times to resume the descent. Go straight across the road, turn left along it, pass a waterpoint and cross the bridge into **Siguer** (toilet on left). Turn right, passing a picnic table, and then left to reach the 'main' street. The GR10 goes straight up the alley. The free gîte d'étape provided by the community is up an alley in the Salle des Fêtes, but no meals are provided. There is one restaurant, Le Café-Rousse, in the village.

FACILITIES FOR STAGE 40

Siguer

There is a free gîte d'étape which does not provide meals. Contact the mairie (town hall) to stay here: tel 05 61 05 65 45

Maison Cancela Accommodation, meals, a small shop and it might be possible to camp on their lawn: tel 07 66 58 17 34, www.maisoncancela.fr

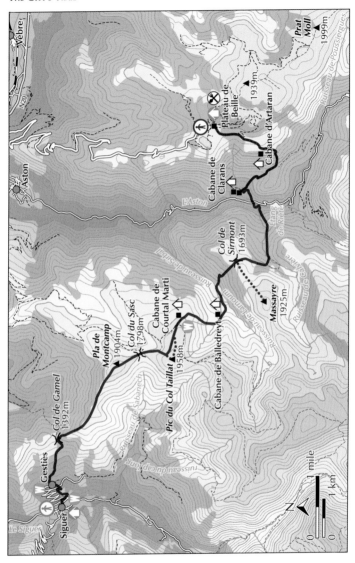

STAGE 41

Siguer to Plateau de Beille

Start	Siguer
Distance	23km
Total ascent	2400m
Total descent	1300m
Time	9hr 40min
High point	Pla de Montcamp (1904m), Col de Sirmont (1693m), Plateau de Beille (1817m)

This stage, with three big climbs, presents a problem for those who require manned accommodation. For those who are not camping, the only option is to break the stage at one of the five bothies on the route. Many of the paths in this stage are a little vague so careful attention to the waymarking will be needed.

Return to the GR10, turn right up the alley and climb. Cross the road three times before arriving at **Gestiès**. Turn right and pass between the church and the waterpoint (35min, 960m). The next water will be at the Cabane de Courtal Marti. Continue climbing, forking right above the hamlet, climbing steeply up an old path and passing several ruined houses before forking left to the **Col de Gamel** (1hr 50min, 1392m). Camping is possible here and on the Crête de la Bède, ahead, but it is far from ideal and there are better sites (equally exposed) between the Pla de Montcamp and the Cabane de Courtal Marti. Turn right, and soon fork left to stay on the ridge. The forest creeps up the slope to your left as you continue up pasture to reach the Col de la Lène (2hr 50min, 1708m). Continue up the ridge to the boulders marking the summit of **Pla de Montcamp** (3hr 35min, 1904m). Paths over the next few hours are rather vague and, although waymarking is sufficient, it does mean there is no room for loss of concentration in mist.

*A horse on Pla
de Montcamp*

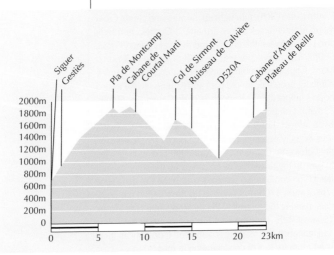

Veer slightly right, passing a newer well-camouflaged cabin and an old cabin before reaching the **Col du Sasc** (1798m). Veer slightly right up a faint path up the ridge and, about 7min later, fork left on an even fainter path which follows a gently rising traverse of the NE slopes of **Pic du Col Taillat** (1959m). ▶

This peak could easily be climbed, rejoining the GR10 by the broad E ridge.

The GR10 reaches the E ridge of Pic du Col Taillat at what is marked on the map as an orri but looks more like an ancient burial mound. Veer left down the ridge and across a track to the **Cabane de Courtal Marti**. The larger first cabin is a berger's hut and the second smaller hut is a very small bothy (4hr 10min, 1812m). About 200m SW of the bothy is a good waterpoint.

Head SW down the ridge to some rocks, veer right and descend steeply to the **Cabane de Balledreyt** (4hr 30min, 1600m).

This bothy was completely renovated in 2014 and provides two rooms for hikers. A supply of basic food items is available here with an honesty box for payment. There is a small stream of dubious quality and reliability about 100m to the W.

Continue down a vague path to the stream and follow it down to reach a bridge over the stream in boggy pasture (5hr 5min). Cross the bridge and go diagonally left to enter the woods and climb a vague steep path up to the broad grassy **Col de Sirmont** (6hr, 1693m) with good campsites. ▶

Massayre (1925m) to the right is an easy peak (up and down in 55min).

The path veers slightly right and begins a descending traverse to the S, which continues through the woods to cross the **Ruisseau de Calvière** (6hr 25min). Descend to the right of the stream. The descent gets steeper as the stream tumbles over waterfalls. Eventually the path crosses the stream on a bridge to reach a track, which is followed down to the D520A road (7hr 10min, 1040m).

Turn right across the bridge and immediately left. Fork right at a junction and climb. The path crosses a small stream and enters a large meadow (7hr 20min).

The Cabane de Clarans is about 150m across the meadow. This small bothy is very basic and mice and rats might be your bed partners. Fortunately, there are good campsites around here. There is also a better second bothy, the Cabane EDF de Clarans. Follow a faint path roughly NNE from the first bothy to reach the second bothy in about 500m.

The GR10 continues up the right-hand side of the meadow and follows a nebulous but well-waymarked path as it climbs through the woods. Eventually you come out on a grassy track where camping would be possible (8hr 20min). Turn left and then veer right to continue climbing until you eventually enter brush. The path gets even vaguer as it climbs to a sign by a large rock (9hr 10min). A sign points to an excellent spring-fed waterpoint about 2min to the right. The GR10 veers left up a small grassy ridge to the **Cabane d'Artaran** (1695m). This bothy was totally renovated in 2018 and even has a bit of artwork on the walls. There are camping opportunities at regular intervals from here until the Refuge du Rulhe at the end of Stage 42.

Veer right along a grassy track, cross a good stream and continue along the track, ignoring turns, until you fork left past the kennels just before the ski complex on the **Plateau de Beille** (9hr 40min, 1817m).

The main building is a bar-restaurant with souvenir shop, toilets and water. On the right, behind the bar-restaurant, is the Angaka Village Nordique. This is an outdoor centre offering mushing in winter and dog-trotting in summer. Excellent accommodation is available for hikers in yurts (Mongolian nomad tents) or teepees. Evening meals are available but need to be booked by 3.00pm as the catering is in conjunction with the restaurant, which is not open in the evening.

FACILITIES FOR STAGE 41

Angaka Village Nordique, Plateau de Beille: tel 05 61 01 75 60, www.angaka.com

STAGE 42

Plateau de Beille to Refuge du Rulhe

Start	Plateau de Beille
Distance	14km
Total ascent	1000m
Total descent	600m
Time	4hr 40min
High point	Crête des Isards (2381m)

Although this is a short stage, it would be advisable to make an early start as the route is along exposed ridges which would be dangerous in an afternoon thunderstorm. This is a spectacular section as you return to the high mountains.

Follow the broad track S from the bar-restaurant, ignoring two right forks. Keep straight on at a major junction and follow the track past the Cabane de Beille-d'en-Haut and descend slightly to a shallow saddle. Continue on

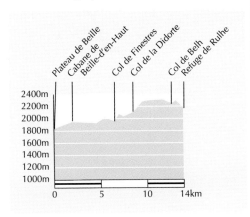

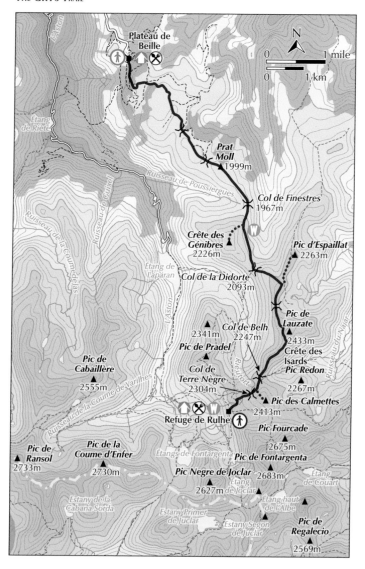

North from Crête des Isards

the track as it goes left of a minor top and then Top 1986 to arrive at a saddle where the dirt track ends (1hr 5min). Follow the grass track SE over the summit of **Prat Moll** (1999m) to another col and over Top 1983 before veering right to the **Col de Finestres** (1hr 35min, 1967m). Climb to a tiny col on the ridge ahead. ▶

The GR10 turns left to traverse the E slopes of the **Crête des Génibres** on a good rough path, which takes you past a cabin (2hr, normally locked) with a good waterpoint. Continue to the **Col de la Didorte** (2hr 25min, 2093m).

The ridge ahead would be a dangerous place in a thunderstorm. The safer option would be to descend SW and then follow the stream S to regain the GR10 at the Col de Terre Nègre.

Veer left up the ridge to a signpost on a minor top (2hr 55min). ▶

You could easily climb Crête des Génibres (2231m) by its NE ridge but pinnacles on the SE ridge prevent a traverse (up and down in 40min).

You could easily climb the twin-summited Pic d'Espaillat (2263m) to the left, NNE, with views down the steep corrie to the NE (up and down in 30min).

249

The GR10 goes right along the ridge, avoiding any difficulties on the right to arrive at a col (3hr 25min). The path now veers right for a rocky traverse of the W face of the **Pic de Lauzate** to arrive at another col. Veer right and traverse the **Crête des Isards**, again avoiding difficulties on the right, to arrive at the **Col de Belh** (4hr 15min, 2247m). Veer slightly right, SW, and climb easily to the **Col de Terre Nègre** (4hr 30min, 2304m). ◀ Descend slightly right, turning left at a junction to reach the **Refuge du Rulhe** (4hr 40min, 2185m). Full refuge facilities including packed lunches. Waterpoint outside.

Pic des Calmettes (2417m) to the left is an easy climb (up and down in 25min).

FACILITIES FOR STAGE 42

Refuge du Rulhe, Rulhe (open late May to late September): tel 05 61 65 65 01 or 06 74 24 50 71 (out of season only), www.rulhe.com

STAGE 43
Refuge du Rulhe to Mérens-les-Vals

Start	Refuge du Rulhe
Distance	12km
Total ascent	500m
Total descent	1600m
Time	4hr 20min
High point	Crête de la Lhasse (2439m)

A short but energetic and scenically impressive stage. Campsites are infrequent on this stage and the first running water is after almost three hours of rough, tough walking in spectacular granite terrain.

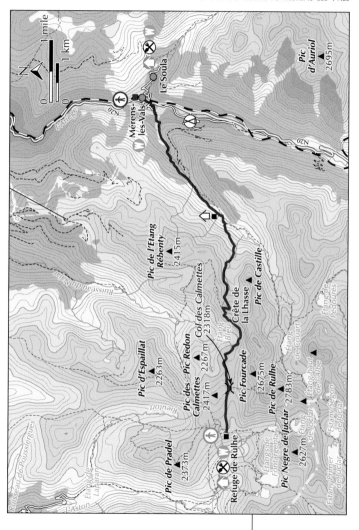

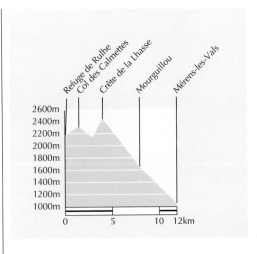

Head E from the refuge and follow a sometimes indistinct path which crosses small boulderfields as it climbs the left-hand side of the valley to arrive just above the **Col des Calmettes** (30min, 2330m). Keep straight on, carefully following waymarks along a rough path and over a boulderfield in complex terrain. Pass round the left-hand side of a small lake (1hr) with one campsite on its E shore. Swimming is easiest from the SW shore. The 'path' heads roughly S then veers back E as it descends to and crosses the outlet stream from the lake. ◀

There follows a generally rising traverse over boulderfields high above the S shore of **Étang Bleu**, a classic corrie lake. The going gets easier as you reach a grassy spur high above the E shore of the lake. A spectacular campsite is possible here. The path now climbs easily up to the ridge of the **Crête de la Lhasse** and follows the ridge a short distance left to a cairn and signpost (2hr 5min, 2439m).

Follow the ridge NE for a further 3min, then switch back into the valley on your right and veer left to descend fairly high up the left-hand side of the valley, avoiding most of the boulderfield. Approach a stream

Although you can hear the stream, you cannot get at the water below the boulderfield.

Pont de Pierres on the descent to Mérens-les-Vals

(2hr 45min). A small but clear path descends to the left of the stream then veers left, passing a small spring-fed stream (2hr 55min) before resuming the descent down to a junction with the path in the Mourguillou Valley (3hr 20min, 1652m). Turn left and pass excellent campsites beside the stream. Just past the pool 'Le Mourguillou' bothy is hidden by bushes just above the path. ▶

The presence of grey heron and dippers seen here suggest good quality water. The pool in the stream, l'Estagnol, is good for a chilly swim.

Continue down the left bank to a stone bridge, Pont de Pierres. Don't cross, but continue, more steeply, down the left-hand side of the stream to the Pont Gazeil (4hr). Cross and continue down an old path on the right-hand side of the stream. Keep straight on across a track and turn right down a road. Follow the road down to the river. The campground is about 15 minutes to the right.

The GR10 goes left to a bridge with a waterpoint (4hr 20min). Cross the bridge into **Mérens-les-Vals** (4hr 20min, 1050m).

The village post office sells a few very basic food items. For a full resupply you will need to take the train to Ax-les-Thermes 9km to the north, where you will find large supermarkets. The SNCF railway station is on the mainline between Latour-de-Carol and Toulouse. L'Auberge du Nabre is 15mins into Stage 44 with the hot springs a further 20min on.

FACILITIES FOR STAGE 43

Mérens-les-Vals

Camping Municipal: tel 05 61 02 85 40, http://camping.merenslesvals.fr

Le Soula

L'Auberge du Nabre, chambres d'hôtes, gîte d'étape, a full meals service and provisions for picnic meals provided: tel 05 61 01 89 36, www.aubergedunabre.com

4 MÉRENS-LES-VALS TO BANYULS-SUR-MER

KEY INFORMATION	
Distance	215km
Total ascent	9700m
Time	65hr walking
Maps	IGN Carte de Randonnées 1:50,000 maps 8, 10, 11

The first few days of this section are through spectacular Alpine terrain before faster progress is made with the Canigou Massif dominating the hills. The terrain becomes drier as the Mediterranean is approached but is still mountainous with the final 1000m peak only being a few miles from Banyuls-sur-Mer. The maps show a multitude of streams in the final stages of this section but most of these are seasonal streams and will be trickling, at best, by the end of summer.

Coma de la Grava (Stage 45)

STAGE 44

Mérens-les-Vals to Refuge des Bésines

Start	Mérens-les-Vals
Distance	10km
Total ascent	1300m
Total descent	300m
Time	4hr 30min
High point	Porteille des Bésines (2333m)

This is a short stage heading back into spectacular but rough Alpine terrain. Allow time to soak in the hot springs above Mérens-les-Vals before tackling the hard stuff.

After crossing the bridge, take care crossing the N20, the main road joining Toulouse to Barcelona, turn left and take the first right, pass under the railway and cross the Nabre. Turn right up the left-hand bank of the stream and continue up the flood wall to reach l'Auberge du

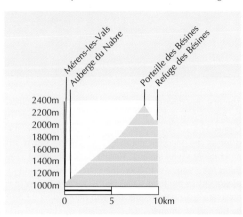

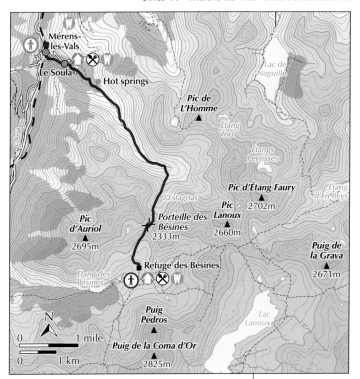

Nabre in **Le Soula** (details in Stage 43). Climb left of the
ruined church and continue uphill (some waymarks missing), then up a track to reach the road by a waterpoint
in Vives, the highest hamlet. Turn right across the stream
and soon turn left up a path between two houses and
climb through the woods. Ignore any side paths to reach
some popular **hot springs** with three small pools (35min).

Continue up a good rocky path through some very
rough terrain. Eventually the path approaches the stream
and you pass a waterfall where swimming in its pool is
possible (1hr 55min). You soon reach good campsites.
Ten minutes later cross the stream on a small bridge and

A ruined church in Le Soula

continue up the right-hand bank, eventually reaching a signpost (2hr 25min, 1832m). Veer right and climb away from the Ruisseau du Nabre and up the right-hand side of a steep v-shaped valley. When the path levels off you could collect water from the stream on your left before veering slightly right up a knoll, which provides a good place to camp (3hr 5min). Just beyond the knoll is a small lake, **l'Estagnas** (2056m), which provides a chilly swim. The path makes a remarkably easy ascent, avoiding virtually all the boulderfields, to arrive at the **Porteille des Bésines** (3hr 55min, 2333m). Descend easily down the left side of the valley, with water and camping to the right. Veer left at a sign and follow waymarks carefully through complex glacial terrain to reach the **Refuge des Bésines** (4hr 30min, 2104m).

The refuge, with a waterpoint, has full refuge facilities, including packed lunches, and it is possible to camp nearby (ask first).

FACILITIES FOR STAGE 44

Refuge des Bésines (open late May to late September): tel 09 88 77 35 28, http://besines.free.fr

STAGE 45
Refuge des Bésines to Refuge des Bouillouses

Start	Refuge des Bésines
Distance	18km
Total ascent	600m
Total descent	700m
Time	5hr 35min
High point	Coll de Coma d'Anyell (2470m), Portella de la Grava (2426m)

This is another very scenic stage that involves crossing two high but easy passes before arriving at the Lac des Bouillouses (La Bollosa), which is a tourist honeypot. There are plenty of good campsites throughout this stage.

Descend left and zigzag down. After a couple of minutes turn sharp left and descend a little further before the path veers left and starts heading ENE up the Coma d'Anyell Valley. The rough, rocky path climbs to the left of the stream before crossing it (45min). Continue climbing. Surprisingly there are campsites and water (1hr 25min) just before you reach the **Coll de Coma d'Anyell** (1hr 40min, 2470m). ▸

The path does not descend immediately, but traverses the S slopes of **Pic Lanoux** (Puig de Lanós) before forking right and descending grassy slopes to cross the outlet stream from the shallow Estany de Lanoset. Round the N tip of **Lac Lanoux** (swimming possible) (2hr

Pic des Bésineilles (2632m) to the right is an easy summit (up and down in 45min); the complex rocky peak to the SE of Lac Lanoux is Pic Carlit (2921m).

259

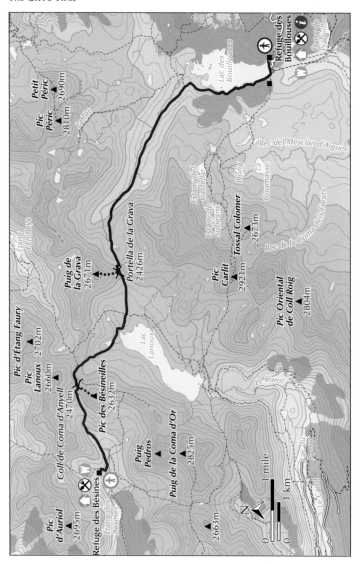

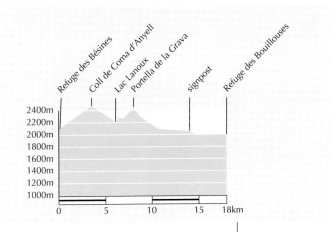

20min, 2213m) and soon veer away from the reservoir. Climb over a small hill to the Cabane du Rouzet, a small berger's cabin. Head E up a gentle grassy valley to the **Portella de la Grava** (3hr 5min, 2426m). ▸ Descend the left-hand side of the valley. Don't worry if you lose the waymarks; just descend to the small l'Estanyol lake where camping and swimming is possible but not ideal because of the cows. After crossing the outlet stream (3hr 20min, 2297m), the path gradually veers right and follows the right-hand side of the long flat Coma de la Grava Valley. Eventually veer right up a slight slope to a signpost (4hr 35min). Keep straight on, climbing slightly before descending to the W shore of the **Lac des Bouillouses**. ▸ Continue along the W shore to reach the dam (5hr 25min, 2020m).

Puig de la Grava (2671m), to the left, is an easy peak and spectacular viewpoint. Follow a faint cairned path (up and down in 60min).

There are places with good swimming where you can dive off rocks into the water.

On the right, just before you reach the dam, is the Hôtel des Bones Hores. There is a tourist office with toilets, a waterpoint and picnic tables at the end of the dam. Camping is only allowed around the lake and to the S of it between 7.00pm and 9.00am.

Puig de la Grava

Cross the dam, or below it if dam gates are locked, to the Auberge du Carlit. The **Refuge des Bouillouses** (5hr 35min, 2010m) is a short distance down the road.

FACILITIES FOR STAGE 45

Tourist office: tel 04 68 04 24 61

Hôtel des Bones Hores, also gîte d'étape accommodation (open mid May to October): tel 04 68 04 24 22, www.boneshores.com

Auberge du Carlit, also gîte d'étape accommodation: tel 04 68 04 22 23, http://lesioux.fr/aubergeducarlit

Refuge des Bouillouses, normal refuge facilities (open June to October): tel 06 86 77 52 82

STAGE 46

Refuge des Bouillouses to Planès

Start	Refuge des Bouillouses
Distance	19km
Total ascent	200m
Total descent	700m
Time	4hr 10min
High point	Refuge des Bouillouses (2010m), Planès (1550m)

This is an easy stage crossing the northeast edge of the high plateau of the Cerdagne, passing accommodation and shops en route. There are plenty of camping opportunities until you are just above Bolquère. The initial sections are complex, with a multitude of trails, so you will need to follow the waymarks carefully.

From the dam, head down the road and turn left between buildings and into the woods. Keep straight on at a junction, veer right to cross the road, fork right, left and right and skirt the woods to arrive at a very basic cabin by the Estany de la Pradella (30min). Follow the track along the S shore, soon forking right away from the lake (this is the best place for swimming). Fork left, ignore a left turn and pass under a chairlift by a clear-looking stream (1hr 5min). Fork right at a junction with a dirt road, left beside a ski lift and follow the track through the woods. Eventually, after reaching the ridge, turn right down a path (immediately after right and left bends in the track) (2hr) and pass the ski chalets of **Pyrénées 2000**. At a complex junction, keep straight on along the path to reach the **D618** road. ▶

Gîte d'etape le Ramiers is 900m to the right.

The GR10 goes straight across the D618 and down the D10C, signed to Bolquère. Pass several picnic sites

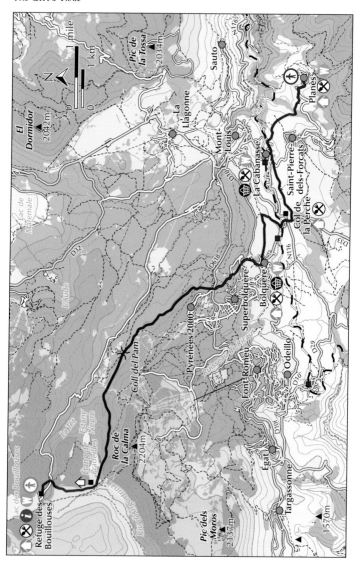

264

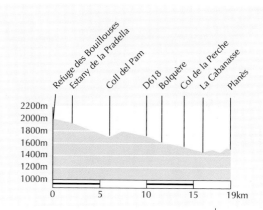

before shortcutting down a missable path after a left-hand bend (2hr 15min). Go straight across a road, then straight on down the road, passing a waterpoint and picnic tables before you arrive at the Place de Ruisseau in the village of **Bolquère** (2hr 30min, 1620m). ▸

The GR10 goes diagonally left from the Place de Ruisseau. On reaching the D10 road, turn left and almost immediately turn left up some steps. Turn left and right along small tarmac roads and you will soon find yourself on a track heading E through fields. Turn right under powerlines and left when you return to the D10. ▸ The GR10 goes left and soon reaches the busy N116 at the **Col de la Perche** (3hr, 1579m). There is a hotel here and the Perpignan to Latour-de-Carol bus passes through.

Cross the N116 and soon turn left along a track, which is followed to the outskirts of **La Cabanasse** (3hr 20min). Turn left along the D32 to arrive in the centre of the village.

There are waterpoints and food shops in the village. The pizzeria/snack bar, which is up the D10 to the left, is probably only open in the evening. Turn right then fork left if you need the main Mont-Louis–La Cabanasse Traine Jaune station. This narrow-gauge

For the small supermarket or accommodation in the village, go straight on up the steps.

The unmanned Train Jaune station, the highest station in France at 1580m, is just up the D10 to the right.

A mural at Mont Louis – La Cabanasse Gare

railway connects with the SNCF network at Latour-de-Carol and Villefranche. Don't think of using the Planès station ahead as it's nowhere near Planès or the GR10!

Turn right, passing a couple of small food shops to reach another waterpoint, then fork right for the GR10 and continue to the bottom of the hill. Turn right down a path. You soon cross a stream. Keep straight on at all junctions as you pass through mixed farmland. Cross another stream (3hr 50min) and climb up to a road. Turn left and enter **Planès**, passing the Chambres d'hôtes Malaza and a waterpoint. Follow the road down and across a stream. ◄ For the GR10, fork right and turn right to the Gîte d'étape l'Orri de Planès (4hr 10min, 1550m).

Fork left for toilets (at the mairie) and for l'Atelier des Sens (opposite the church) with a snack bar which sells quality bread and limited groceries.

FACILITIES FOR STAGE 46

Bolquère

Gîte d'étape Les Ramiers, gîte d'étape, chambres d'hôtes accommodation and meal service: tel 04 68 30 37 48, www.lesramiers.fr

Hôtel-restaurant le Lassus: tel 09 74 56 14 70, www.restaurant-lassus.fr

Hôtel-restaurant l'Ancienne Auberge: tel 04 68 30 09 51, www.hotel-pyrenees2000.fr

Col de la Perche

Hôtel le Catalan: tel 04 68 04 21 83, www.hotellecatalan.com

Planès

Gîte d'étape l'Orri de Planès, gîte d'étape and chambres d'hôtes accommodation with full meals service, picnic lunches, camping area and swimming pool. Coming under new ownership in 2023: tel 04 68 04 29 47 or www.orrideplanes.com

Chambres d'hôtes Malaza: tel 06 66 29 03 79, https://chambre-dhotes-le-malaza.business.site

STAGE 47

Planès to Refuge du Ras de la Carança

Start	Planès
Distance	15km
Total ascent	1200m
Total descent	900m
Time	5hr 45min
High point	Pla de Cédeilles (1911m), Col Mitja (2367m)

This stage is an easy crossing of the Col Mitja. An early start is recommended as this mountain range seems to attract more than its fair share of afternoon thunderstorms.

Continue up the road, pass a waterpoint, fork right, turn left up a path and then right up a track to a track junction.

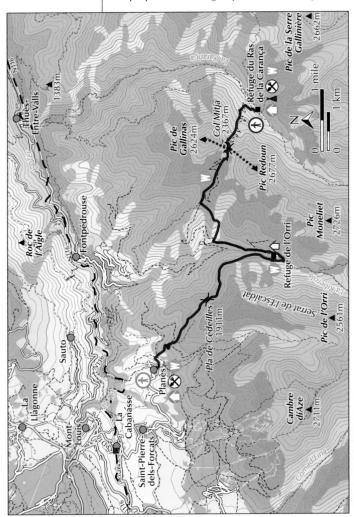

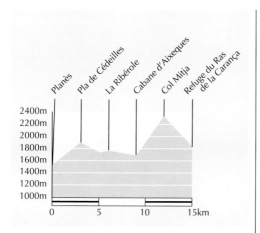

Keep straight on up a good path which is followed to cross a track (30min) and climb easily to the **Pla de Cédeilles** (1hr 5min, 1911m) on the N ridge of Pic de l'Orri (2561m). ▶ The path traverses right from the col, with ups and downs, and enters the Ribérole Valley. Climb gently up the valley to a bridge by an orri at Jaça Grossa (2hr 15min, 1826m) where there are good campsites.

Cross the bridge and descend to the **Refuge de l'Orri** (2hr 25min). This berger's cabin has a waterpoint and the right-hand room is available as a bothy for hikers. Descend the grassy track, high above la Ribérole. Cross a side stream before reaching a junction with a bigger track (2hr 40min). Fork right and soon reach the tiny Cabane d'Aixeques (1688m), which could be used for an emergency bivouac, but you wouldn't likely set out with the intention of using it as it's very basic (it doesn't even have a door). Turn right off the track to the right of a fenced enclosure and climb and head up a small, but clear path over rough open terrain on the left-hand side of the Aychéques Valley. Eventually veer left, cross a ridge and climb through woods to reach a track (3hr 45min) with good campsites.

Fork right, then keep straight on at a right-hand switchback in the track and climb through pasture and

This shallow grassy saddle provides excellent campsites with good views of Pic de Gallinas and Pic Redoun ahead.

269

Cerdagne from Pic de Gallinas

Pic de Gallinas (2624m) to the left and Pic Redoun (2677m) to the right are both worthwhile climbs (both take 75min there and back).

open woodland. Springwater from a pipe provides good water (4hr 10min). Cross the track twice and then go left along it before shortcutting right to the grassy **Col Mitja** (4hr 55min, 2367m) with good but exposed campsites. ◄ The GR10 zigzags down a path, frequently crossing the switchbacking track as it descends a rough open slope. Once the gradient eases the GR10 goes straight down the slope, crossing the track on a number of occasions before following it right to the **Refuge du Ras de la Carança** (5hr 45min, 1831m).

The refuge has a waterpoint, aire de bivouac and full refuge facilities including picnic lunches.

FACILITIES FOR STAGE 47

Refuge du Ras de la Carança (open late May to late September): tel 09 88 67 73 81, www.refugelacaranca.com

STAGE 48

Refuge du Ras de la Carança to Mantet

Start	Refuge du Ras de la Carança
Distance	11km
Total ascent	600m
Total descent	900m
Time	4hr
High point	Coll del Pal (2294m), Serre de Caret (2300m)

The Coll del Pal is another easy pass but care will be needed with navigation as the path isn't always well defined and the waymarking is below normal GR10 standards; it is sufficient to follow the route, but not enough to be confident you are doing so!

Continue upstream from the refuge, soon turning left across a bridge and climbing away from the stream. Veer left when you reach the foot of the meadows of the Pla de Bassibès (20min). Cross the last stream on the ascent and descend gently through woods, gradually veering right and starting to climb. Leave the woods (45min) and enter the Réserve Naturelle de Mantet, the designation of which seems incompatible with the high concentration of cows in the area. There are 'no camping' signs, but bivouac is allowed between 7.00pm and 9.00am. Climb roughly SE up pasture and open woodland, veering right beneath some crags and boulderfields. Eventually

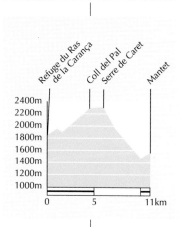

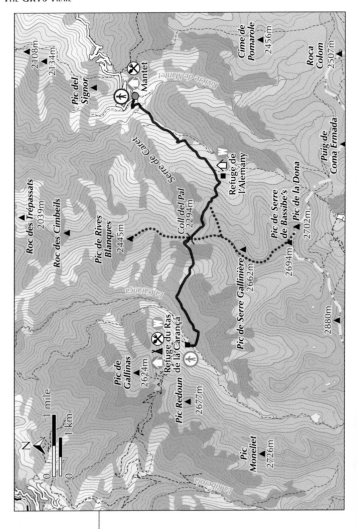

veer left to a gate (1hr 25min) and climb through woods
veering left to emerge at the grassy slopes below the

Looking back to Coll Mitja from the climb to Coll del Pal

Coll del Pal. Continue up to the col (2hr, 2294m) with exposed campsites. ▶

You get your first good view ahead to the dominating Pic du Canigou (2784m).

> From here you could climb **Pic de Serre Gallinère** (2663m), on the right (up and down in 100min). You could continue to **Pic de Serre de Bassibès** (2694m) (up and down in 145min) or even onto **Pic de la Dona** (2702m) on the border ridge (up and down in 180min). **Pic de Rives Blanques** (2445m) to the left is also an option. A Patou sheepdog has been known to 'guard' this area so be cautious if you encounter one.

Don't descend, but contour right. After 4mins cross a small stream (can be dry by late summer) fed by a spring well up the hillside. Continue contouring to arrive at the grassy **Serre de Caret** ridge (2hr 20min, 2300m). ▶ Keep straight on and descend steeply through rough open terrain, veering left to a junction as the gradient eases (2hr 55min, 1960m).

You could also climb Pic de Serre Gallinère from here.

The Refuge de l'Alemany is a few minutes to the right. This bothy, with a waterpoint and toilet, is in excellent condition.

The GR10 goes left and descends easily, picking up an old path lower down the valley to reach a bridge over the Rivière de l'Alemany (3hr 45min). Cross and veer away from the stream, then ford the Rivière de Ressec (there is a bridge downstream) and follow the track, forking right into **Mantet** (4hr, 1550m).

Gîte d'étape la Girada and Gîte à la ferme Cazenove are at the bottom of the hamlet. Auberge la Bouf' Tic is at the top of the hamlet and Gîte d'étape la Cavale is a short distance into the next stage.

FACILITIES FOR STAGE 48

Mantet

Gîte d'étape la Girada: tel 04 68 05 68 69

Gîte à la Ferme Cazenove, chambres d'hôtes: tel 04 68 05 60 99, www.gitecazenovemantet.fr

Auberge la Bouf' Tic, chambres d'hôtes with bar-restaurant: tel 04 68 05 51 76, http://aubergelabouftic.wix.com/auberge-mantet

Gîte d'étape la Cavale, gîte d'étape and chambres d'hôtes accommodation with riding centre: tel 04 68 05 57 59, http://la-cavale.fr

STAGE 49

Mantet to Refuge de Mariailles

Start	Mantet
Distance	15km
Total ascent	1100m
Total descent	900m
Time	5hr 15min
High point	Col de Mantet (1761m), Refuge de Mariailles (1718m)

After the easy crossing of the Col de Mantet the GR10 descends to Py, where there is accommodation and a small epicerie, before the long climb to the Refuge de Mariailles.

Continue up through Mantet, passing a public toilet and the Auberge la Bouf' Tic. Turn sharp right at the top of the hamlet and then switch back left up a path as you

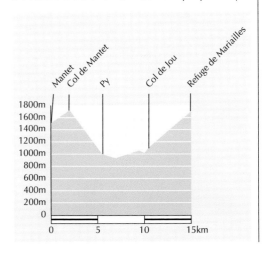

approach the Gîte d'étape la Cavale (see Stage 48 for details). The path zigzags up the hill, briefly going right up the D6 road before resuming the climb up the path to the D6 at the **Col de Mantet** (40min, 1761m) where there are unusual sculptures, information boards and a car park.

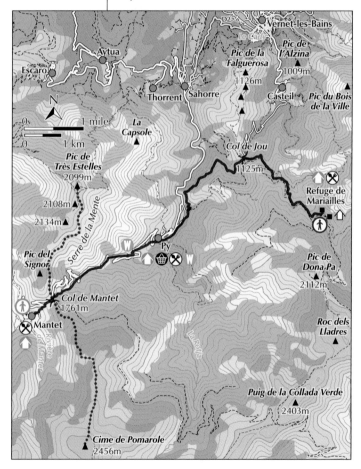

Sculpture at Col de Mantet

From the Col de Mantet one path heads N along the E slopes of the ridge to **Pic de Très Estelles** (2099m) giving superb views of Canigou (up and down in 130min). Another path heads S to **Cime de Pomarole** (2456m) and on to **Roc Colom** (2507m) on the border. These mountains are part of a vast grassy plateau.

The GR10 follows a good path, which winds down to the right of the D6, returning to it by a small woodland stream. There are a few possible campsites on this descent. Follow the road a short distance then take a couple of shortcuts on the right, passing a surprising spring-fed waterpoint and then la Meridienne Verte (1hr 25min), which marks the tree-planting effort in 2000 along the meridian through Paris. Go straight across the road three times before arriving at the centre of **Py** (1hr 50min, 1023m).

In Py you will find l'Auberge de Py with a bar-restaurant and an epicerie with a small selection of food. If the epicerie is closed, ask at the bar for it to be opened. The waterpoint and gîte d'étape are in the centre of the hamlet. There is a bus service to Prades.

Continue down the road, forking right and keeping straight on as the road deteriorates to a track before returning to the D6 at the edge of the village. After crossing a bridge, fork right along the Cami de la Farga and through la Farga (940m). Soon, fork right up a path, which is rough in places, for a rising traverse across steep slopes. Reach a ridge (2hr 50min, 1064m) and veer right, descending a little to cross a small woodland stream before climbing to the **Col de Jou** (3hr 25min, 1125m). Here you will find a car park and a small stream with waterfalls, which could provide a refreshing shower. This col provides the first campsites since Py but the setting beside dirt roads is far from ideal.

Veer right, crossing the dirt road, and climb a smaller track past water tanks before climbing steadily to a car park with a leat (channelled stream) (3hr 55min). Follow the lower of the left-hand paths as it climbs steeply to reach a rocky ridge at a small col. You could camp here, but there are better sites ahead. Continue up the ridge to the Col du Cheval Mort (4hr 25min, 1456m). Keep straight on along or below the leat to reach a ruin where camping is possible. Switch back right, returning to the leat before climbing away from it to cross another little col before regaining the leat. Eventually leave it and climb to meadows and the **Refuge de Mariailles** (5hr 15min, 1718m).

The refuge has full facilities including packed lunches.

FACILITIES FOR STAGE 49

Py

Gîte d'étape de Py 'La Casa Sant Pau', accommodation, no meals: tel 06 16 11 56 53 or 06 41 87 57 60

Auberge de Py, chambres d'hôtes: tel 04 68 04 12 26, www.auberge-de-py.business.site

Stage end

Refuge de Mariailles (manned mid May to late October, open all year): tel 04 68 05 57 99, www.refugedemariailles.fr

STAGE 50

Refuge de Mariailles to Refuge des Cortalets

Start	Refuge de Mariailles
Distance	18km
Total ascent	1000m
Total descent	600m
Time	5hr 55min; alternative route 5hr 25min
High point	NE ridge of Pic Joffre (2250m)

This stage follows the Tour du Canigou as it traverses the north slopes of the Pic du Canigou (2784m). For most of this stage you are following good mountain paths through difficult, rough terrain. When the weather is good, it is recommended that you leave the GR10 to traverse this iconic Catalan mountain.

Climb SSE from the refuge to a car park with bothy on the left. The GR10 then follows the path forking left below the leat, soon passing a picnic site with waterpoint. Continue

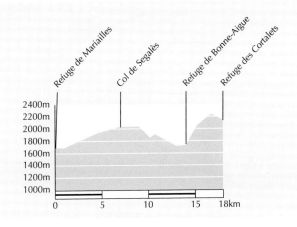

contouring to a bridge over a stream and then start climbing gently. Pass a small pipe with springwater (1hr 5min) and continue to cross the **Torrent de Cady** (1hr 20min) and veer left to a path junction below the Roc de Cady (1hr 35min, 2022m).

Via the Pic du Canigou
In good weather it is recommended that you turn right here and follow a good path (yellow waymarks) past **Abri Aragó**, a small bothy, with a waterpoint and good campsites (1hr 55min). Cross a small stream (2hr 20min) and start zigzagging up the W slopes of **Puig Sec**. Pass an excellent waterpoint on a switchback (2hr 50min). Eventually the path heads NNW. Fork left and follow a rocky path to the foot of the S wall of **Pic du Canigou**. This may look daunting, but it is not much more than a steep staircase with a bit of easy scrambling. Arrive at the summit (2784m; 4hr 10min), which is a pilgrimage point for the Catalans.

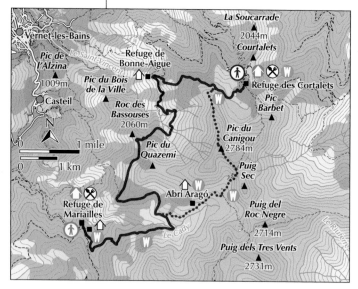

The descent down the N ridge is easy. Follow the path passing a waterpoint a minute before the junction with the GR10 (5hr 5min), which is followed to the **Refuge des Cortalets** (5hr 25min).

The summit of Pic du Canigou

Turn left for the GR10 and climb to round the ridge and reach a path junction, signed Col de Segalès (2hr 5min, 2040m). This junction isn't at a col so the name may refer to the col where you cross the rocky ridge ahead. Continue to reach the Col de la Jasse d'en Vernet, to the right of the **Roc des Bassouses** (2hr 40min). Veer right and descend a little before crossing a dry, boulder-filled valley and descending on a rough path. Pass the Font d'Escureo water source (3hr 20min). This spring, or a couple of small streams ahead, will be your only water before the Refuge des Cortalets, but they could dry up in a hot summer.

Arrive at the switchback of a track at Jasse del Py (3hr 45min, 1749m). Fork right along the track to the recently renovated **Refuge de Bonne-Aigue** (4hr, 1730m).

This basic bothy was in good condition in 2022. There is no waterpoint at the bothy but if you continue 400m along the track the Bonne-Aigue stream may be running. Camping is possible, cows permitting!

Continue along the track, forking right after 100m and then climbing a good mountain path up the ridge to an orri in pasture (4hr 40min). This could be used for an emergency bivouac and you should be able to find a flat enough spot to camp. Soon, veer left to a ridge and then veer right for a rising traverse of the N slopes of the ridge where you will get your first view of the Mediterranean beyond the city of Perpignan. Continue climbing to a junction with the main path descending from the Pic du Canigou (5hr 35min, 2784m). There is a waterpoint about a minute up this path. Turn left and descend to a stagnant lake, passing left of it to reach the **Refuge des Cortalets** (5hr 55min, 2150m). ◄

If you didn't traverse the Pic du Canigou you might like to climb it by its NNW ridge from here (up and down in about 150min).

Refuge des Cortalets is a CAF refuge with full refuge facilities and a waterpoint outside. If you want to camp you may do so between the refuge and the lake.

FACILITIES FOR STAGE 50

Refuge des Cortalets (manned late May to mid October, open year round): tel 04 68 96 36 19, https://refugedescortalets.ffcam.fr

STAGE 51

Refuge des Cortalets to Gîte-refuge de Batère

Start	Refuge des Cortalets
Distance	17km
Total ascent	300m
Total descent	900m
Time	4hr 15min; alternative route 4hr 30min
High point	Refuge des Cortalets (2150m)

There would be time for a strong walker to climb Canigou in the morning before walking this easy stage. The higher variation, following the Tour du Canigou, is well waymarked and is now considered to be the main route.

High route via the Tour du Canigou

Go right from behind the refuge, soon forking left. ▶ Eventually the path leaves the forest and veers right, S, before switching back and descending the ridge E down to rejoin the GR10 at Ras del Prat Cabrera (1hr 15min, 1739m).

The right fork climbs Canigou by the Crête de Barbet.

Refuge des Cortalets

The alternative route rejoins here from back right.

From Refuge des Cortalets the GR10 follows a good path NE from the refuge before turning right down a dirt road to arrive at a road junction. Turn right, passing a waterpoint, and follow the road to a switchback at the Ras del Prat Cabrera (1hr, 1739m). ◄

Turn right and follow a path on a gently descending traverse. Cross three streams at the head of the Lentilla Valley (1hr 25min) and continue the traverse to arrive at the **Abri du Pinatell** (2hr, 1680m). Structurally in good condition, this bothy was nevertheless closed for much of 2021 and 2022 due to a bed bug infestation! There is a waterpoint and picnic table outside. Continue contouring, then zigzag down to the **Refuge de l'Estanyol** (2hr 35min, 1479m). This bothy, also with a waterpoint and picnic table, is in excellent condition.

Continue a short distance to a col where there are good campsites. Veer right and climb on a good path. Cross a small stream and continue to the **Col de la Cirère**

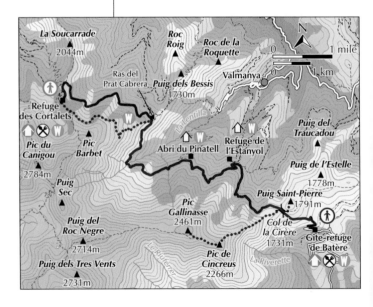

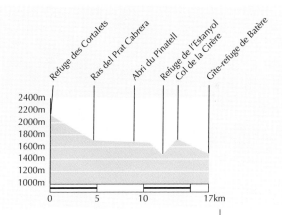

(3hr 45min, 1731m). You could camp at the col but there is more sheltered camping in the quarries ahead.

> **Puig Saint-Pierre** (1791m), to the left, is an easy summit (up and down in 15min). A path is shown on the map heading W over Puig del Peldecà (2105m) and Pic de Cincreus (2266m) to Pic Gallinasse (2461m).

Descend left from the col, pass old mines and quarries and then veer right down a grassy ridge. Pass a ruined farmhouse and then turn right down a track before zigzagging down and joining the D43 road. Pass some derelict buildings before reaching the **Gîte-refuge de Batère** with a waterpoint outside (4hr 15min, 1470m).

FACILITIES FOR STAGE 51

Gîte-refuge de Batère, chambres d'hôtes, gîte d'étape accommodation, full meals service and hot tub (manned April to early November, open year round): tel 07 57 67 31 71, www.gite-refuge-batere.com

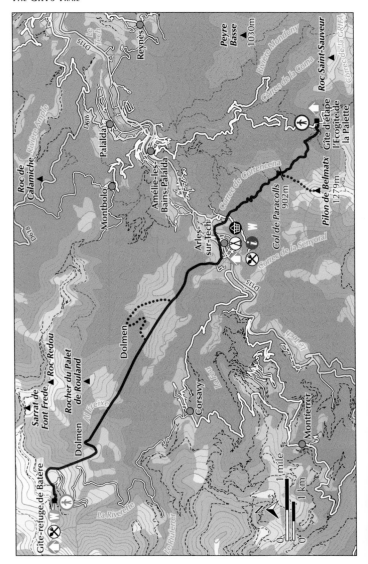

STAGE 52

Gîte-refuge de Batère to Gîte d'étape l'Ecogîte de la Palette

Start	Gîte-refuge de Batère
Distance	19km
Total ascent	700m
Total descent	1500m
Time	6hr 10min
High point	Gîte-refuge de Batère (1470m), Col de Paracolls (902m)

This stage is a long descent to cross the valley of Le Tech at Arles-sur-Tech, followed by a climb of the Col de Paracolls.

Continue down the D43 to the Col de la Descarga (1393m). Keep straight on down a grassy path beside a small stream with a few possible campsites. Soon, veer right back onto the ridge and follow it steeply down to cross a track (45min). There is good camping just ahead at the Collada del Roure (1031m). Continue down a track, passing a well-preserved **dolmen** on a knoll in the woods to the left of the track. There are good campsites nearby.

When the track switches back left (1hr 5min) keep straight on along a path, passing an old workshop, Els Vigorats (884m), where you could bivouac. Go straight across a track and cross a stream with a rockpool (1hr 20min) with good camping just beyond. Turn right and then right along a track, ignoring a path forking right. Then fork right, turn right and fork right. ▶ Turn right down a path, turn right and fork right at an old workshop, le Moulinet (2hr 5min). This workshop, some other buildings and the remains of a bucket lift date back to the heyday of the mining industry. The path descends a stony ridge and joins a track at a shallow saddle with the last

Rather than fork right, you could continue along the track and just after a left-hand bend is a sign to a well-preserved dolmen. After this, return to the GR10 on the ridge by taking every right turn.

A dolmen on the descent to Arles-sur-Tech

scruffy campsites on the descent (2hr 30min). Soon, turn right down a path to arrive at a concrete track on the edge of the small town of **Arles-sur-Tech**. Turn left to a road.

Turn right if you want Camping du Riuferrer. The GR10 goes left and then forks left down a road closed to traffic. Go straight on past three schools and down an alley, the Traverse Albert Rouge, to reach a road (2hr 55min, 280m).

> You will probably want to turn right and left for the Spar supermarket and the tourist office, which is in the Abbaye. The supermarket sells original and easy-clic camping gas.

Turn left to follow the GR10 and then turn right down an alley, the Passage de la Coquinière. Keep straight on past the old railway station and bus stops. There is a regular bus service to Perpignan. Pass toilets with water and veer left down a track. Turn left to cross le Tech on a long footbridge and keep straight on before forking right and veering right, out of the woods into a meadow where camping would be possible. Follow the waymarks carefully over the lower section of the ascent, which is vague and complex.

When you reach a road turn right, shortcut left, then turn left up the road and left up a path. Fork right at a junction and climb steeply up a clear rocky path. Eventually

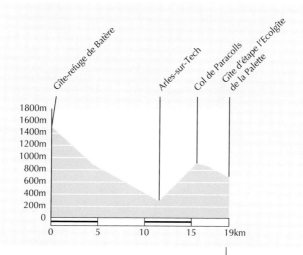

you will reach a junction (4hr 50min). Fork right to reach the **Col de Paracolls** (5hr 5min, 902m). ▶ Keep straight on along a path which traverses the NE slopes of the **Pilon de Belmatx**. Cross a stream that is often pretty lacklustre by late summer (5hr 20min) and reach a col with the ruins of Paracolls farm. This col provides your first good campsites since Arles. Contour before descending to another unreliable stream (5hr 50min) and climbing before the final descent to a bigger stream. Cross and veer left to the **Gîte d'étape l'Ecogîte de la Palette** (6hr 10min, 661m).

You could climb Pilon de Belmatx (1280m) by its NE ridge from here following red/yellow waymarks. This rocky summit, topped by a Catalan flag, is an excellent viewpoint (up and down 85min).

FACILITIES FOR STAGE 52

Arles-sur-Tech

Tourist office: tel 04 68 39 11 99, www.tourisme-haut-vallespir.com

Gîte d'étape l'Ecogîte de la Palette, full meals service, using locally produced organic food, supplies for picnic lunches, an aire de bivouac as well as refreshing rockpools in the river: tel 04 68 21 37 24, http://ecogitedetape66.com

The Gîte d'étape des Glycines, near the Spar supermarket, was closed for the 2022 season, but there's no information whether it will re-open in the future.

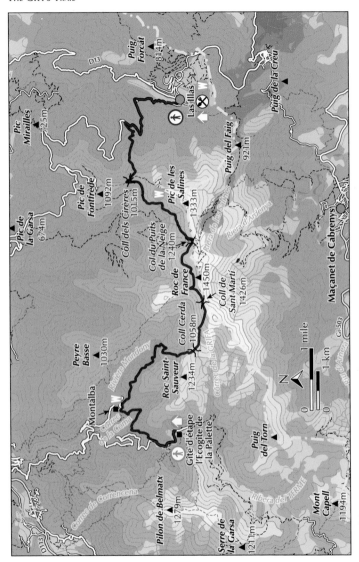

STAGE 53

Gîte d'étape l'Ecogîte de la Palette to Las Illas

Start	Gîte d'étape l'Ecogîte de la Palette
Distance	22km
Total ascent	1000m
Total descent	1100m
Time	7hr
High point	Coll de Sant Martí (1426m)

The mountains are getting lower, and the sense of an approaching Mediterranean stronger but, if anything, the mountains are getting steeper as the GR10 follows forest paths up to the border ridge on the west ridge of Roc de France (Roc de Frausa) before descending to Las Illas. These steep, rocky forests are full of wildlife including lots of wild boar and, if you set off early, you might be lucky enough to spy one.

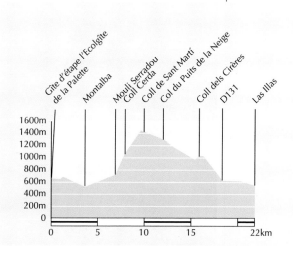

The GR10 goes right of the gîte d'étape to the D536 road. Turn left and follow the road for about 1km before forking right up a path. Traverse the slopes of the NW ridge of Roc St-Sauveur (1235m) to reach **Montalba** (55min, 543m) where there is an unreliable waterpoint. Turn sharp right at the cross above the hamlet and climb. Fork left (1hr 25min) and then fork right when you reach a switchback in a track (1hr 45min). Pass a couple of trickling streams, which could be dry by late summer. Fork right (camping possible here) and cross another, possibly dry, stream and start climbing steeply. Soon, pass the ruins of Mouli Serradou (2hr 20min, 833m) and keep climbing to reach **Coll Cerda** (2hr 45min, 1058m) with the first good campsites on this stage.

Turn left and continue climbing, eventually to reach a trickling stream, which also may be dry. Cross the stream (3hr 15min) and continue climbing to approach the ridge

The west ridge of Roc de France

before traversing left to reach a point a few metres below the **Coll de Sant Martí** (3hr 50min, 1426m) on the rocky west ridge of Roc de France. ▶

The GR10 soon reaches a fork as it re-enters the woods. The right fork is followed by the HRP, which climbs over the Roc de France, while we follow the GR10 left along an easier path which traverses the N slopes of the **Roc de France**.

A few minutes later pass good campsites on a grassy ridge and then fork right, continuing to the **Col du Puits de la Neige** (4hr 30min, 1240m), which has good camping. Pay careful attention to the waymarking on the descent to Las Illas as the route is complex. Do not cross the col but descend left of the rocks and start a tough traverse with ups, as well as downs, on a rough rocky path. A spring-fed pipe may provide water (5hr 10min), but in hot summers it can run dry. Fifteen minutes later fork right and eventually arrive at a wooded col. Cross the col, turn right and contour to the **Coll dels Cirères** (5hr 40min, 1015m). Fork left to a third col, with better camping, and then veer left to start the descent. After crossing a couple of tracks, turn left and zigzag down to la Selva farmhouse. After a couple more switchbacks, you reach the D13F road (6hr 15min).

Turn right and follow the road to a junction at the edge of Las Illas. ▶ Turn right for the centre of **Las Illas**, pass a picnic site with a waterpoint and toilets and then turn right for the gîte d'étape, which is by the mairie (7hr, 550m).

The guardian for the village-run gîte d'étape lives across the road. This gîte d'étape has no meals service, but meals can be obtained from the Hostal des Trabucayres, a basic hotel with bar-restaurant, just up the road.

The rare black-winged kite has been sighted here – a small grey and white raptor with black shoulders. It's actually native to North Africa but has recently started spreading through Spain and southern France.

If you don't want the facilities of Las Illas you should turn left now.

FACILITIES FOR STAGE 53

Las Illas

Gîte d'étape las Illas: tel 07 76 09 65 81

Hostal dels Trabucayres, simple rooms and good meals: tel 04 68 66 55 38, www.facebook.com/trabucayres

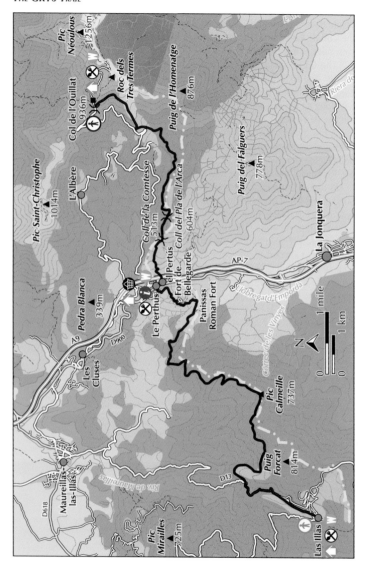

STAGE 54

Las Illas to Col de l'Ouillat

Start	Las Illas
Distance	27km
Total ascent	1000m
Total descent	600m
Time	6hr 15min
High point	Pic Calmeille (737m), Col de l'Ouillat (936m)

The penultimate day is a long one, but the path carries you through diverse landscapes and past several sites of historical interest. Waymarking can be a little sparse in places so pay attention at junctions. The border town of Le Perthus has only very limited accommodation. There are plenty of places to camp in this stage.

Return to the road junction and head N along the **D13**, ignoring two right turns and a track forking right before turning right up a forest road (35min). Five minutes later fork right and then turn left. Cross a possibly dry, trickling

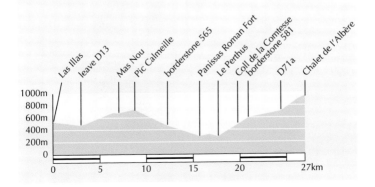

stream and continue to a track junction (1hr 25min). Turn left and pass Mas Nou farmhouse. There is a sign asking you to stay on the track through the private property of a naturist community and the militia-style security will ensure you respect the rules! Turn right and follow the track as it climbs to the border ridge and follow it, passing plenty of good campsites.

Follow the track, ignoring all side turns to borderstone 565 (2hr 30min). Five minutes later turn right up a small path through the cork forest, turn right along a concrete track and pass Mas Bardes farmhouse. The track becomes a small tarmac road to arrive at the **Panissas Roman Fort** (3hr).

An old fort on Col de Panissas

The Romans constructed the **Via Domitia** in 118BC along the line of the ancient route that Hannibal had followed when he invaded Italy. The Panissas Fort was built on the border between Spain and Gaul to protect the vulnerable crossing of the Pyrenees. The Roman road continues into Spain as the Via Augusta, terminating at Cadiz.

Continue along the road. As you cross the Col de Panissas, you will see an old fort on the ridge on your right and pass a seventeenth-century military cemetry before turning left immediately before the **Fort de Bellegarde**.

Le Perthus became French territory after the **Treaty of the Pyrenees** in 1659 leading to the need to protect this important pass. The original fort at Bellegarde was captured by the Spaniards in 1674, but retaken by the French in 1675. In 1678 the French started building the new Fort de Bellegarde, which dominates the area today.

Pass a tiny shelter and follow the road into **Le Perthus** (3hr 30min, 290m). The tourist office is on the corner with a waterpoint opposite.

Le Perthus is a curious border town, partly French and partly Spanish. If you head down the main street you pass small tourist shops and bar-restaurants/snack bars. You then pass borderstone 576 and immediately there is a Spanish supermarket, and a plethora of tourist shops, at Spanish prices. The French cannot compete against the lower taxes on food and alcohol in Spain.

The GR10 goes left from the tourist office before turning right by a large car park and following the road under the **motorway**. Almost immediately fork right up a track and after two switch backs fork left up a path and enter Spain. The path becomes a track by the time you switch back left at a junction (3hr 50min), fork right, switch back left and then right by a farm building. Fork left up a path and re-enter France at the **Coll de la Comtesse** by borderstone 580 (4hr 20min, 513m).

You soon fork right along a forest road and turn left at the **Coll del Pla de l'Arca** by borderstone 581 (604m). Next fork left and cross a couple of streams, which may be dry. Turn right up the second stream (5hr 5min). Soon, veer left and climb, turning right and left. When you approach the D71a road above St-Martin-de-l'Albère, veer right and turn left up a grassy track. Turn right and almost immediately fork right up a path, cross a track and leave the wood (5hr 35min). Continue climbing through brush, eventually fork left and re-enter the forest for a rising traverse to the Chalet de l'Albère at the **Col de l'Ouillat** (6hr 15min, 936m). There is a waterpoint about 120m along the road to the right.

FACILITIES FOR STAGE 54

Le Perthus

Gîte d'étape Chez Paco: tel 06 13 09 89 36, www.chezpaco.e-monsite.com

Chambre d'hôte Chez Grand-Mère, the best option in the village: tel 04 68 67 35 77, www.chezgrandmere-leperthus.com

Col de l'Ouillat

Chalet de l'Albère, gîte d'étape with bar-restaurant, picnic lunches can be provided and it is possible to bivouac at the picnic site across the road: tel 04 68 83 62 20, https://chalet-de-lalbere.fr

STAGE 55

Col de l'Ouillat to Banyuls-sur-Mer

Start	Col de l'Ouillat
Distance	24km
Total ascent	700m
Total descent	1600m
Time	6hr 50min
High point	Pic Néulos (1257m)

The final stage of the GR10 follows the border ridge for a considerable distance before the final descent to Banyuls-sur-Mer. These are grassy mountains with woods encroaching from the flanks and plenty of rock outcrops. On the frontier, peaks and cols will generally have French, Spanish and Catalan names and there is further confusion with Spanish signposts, which refer to routes in Spain. It is possible to camp almost anywhere along the ridge until you start the final descent from the Pic de Sailfort. The GR10 skirts left of most of the summits on the ridge, but it is possible follow the border over the summits.

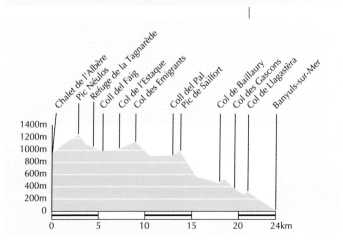

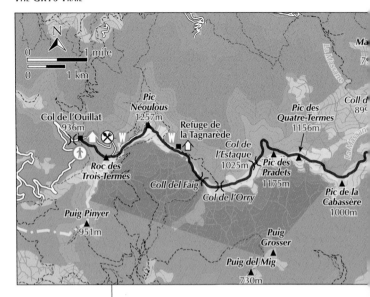

Turn sharp right from the Chalet de l'Albère and climb the NW ridge of the **Roc des Trois-Termes** (1128m), veering left to a shallow saddle to the NE of the summit. Follow the border fence roughly NE, veering left immediately before the tall summit cairn on **Pic Néulos** (1hr 5min, 1257m). Cross the road and follow the track around the communications complex and descend almost S, veering SE down to the Font de la Tagnarède, which is well below the ridge. This is likely to be your only water until you reach the vineyards above Banyuls. Unless you have confirmed that this spring is running it would be sensible to carry water from the Chalet de l'Albère. Follow the path which contours from the waterpoint to the **Refuge de la Tagnarède** (1hr 30min, 1045m). Structurally, this eight-bed bothy is in good condition, but the intensely graffitied walls rather diminish the experience of staying here. Continue contouring, then veer right onto the ridge and follow it. Pass the **Coll del Faig** (985m) and grassy **Col de l'Orry** before climbing the Puig de las Basses. There is no path in this

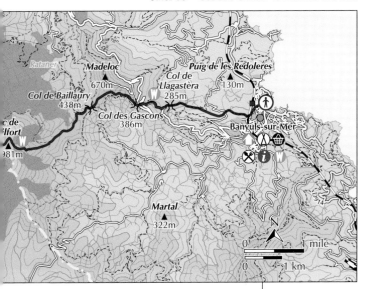

area so care will be needed, in mist, to follow the way-marks which are supplemented by cairns. The 'path' levels off and passes borderstone 586 to reach the shallow

Border stone 586

Sunrise from camp on Pic des Quatre-Termes

Col de l'Estaque (2hr 25min, 1025m). Follow the faint path diagonally left, leading to a good path through the woods before veering right round the N ridge of the **Pic des Pradets** (1175m) to return to the border ridge.

Skirt left of the **Pic des Quatre-Termes** (1156m) and veer right to stay on, or just left of, the main ridge. Skirt the N slopes of the **Pic de la Cabassère**, returning to the ridge before veering left round the next top to reach the **Coll del Pal** (3hr 55min, 899m) with borderstone 589 carved into a rock outcrop. Climb the shallow col between the two tops of the **Pic de Sailfort** (4hr 10min, 981m) where you have your last good campsites on the GR10 as well as your first view of Banyuls-sur-Mer.

Descend a short distance and then veer right along a rough rocky path to reach the Serrat du Castell Serradillou. Descend this ridge, soon passing a signpost for 'source'. Follow red dots a short distance left for a spring. Eventually veer left to a signpost (4hr 50min, 554m). Turn right along a better path, ignore a path to the left, pass under a pow-erline and join a track to arrive at the **Col de Baillaury** (5hr

15min, 438m). Fork left along a path which climbs the ridge to the Col de Formigou (5hr 30min). Cross and traverse the S-facing slopes before veering right for the short descent to the road at the **Col des Gascons** (5hr 50min, 386m). Keep straight on down the road, soon shortcutting left down a path. Go straight across the road at the next two crossings and pass a waterpoint.

Turn left down the road, descending through vineyards to reach the **Col de Llagastèra** (285m). Take the right-hand of the two E tracks, fork right at a junction, then fork right, right again, turn sharp right, switch back left and then fork right down a path by some animal enclosures. Join a track and immediately turn right along a path. Fork left, go straight across a road and fork right. Fork right and turn left along a road under the **railway**. The station is to the left, but the GR10 goes straight on down an alley. Turn left, then left and right past Banyuls l'Etoile winery to arrive at the seafront in **Banyuls-sur-Mer** (6hr 50min). Put down your bag. Remove your boots. Dive into the warm Mediterranean. You've done it!

> There is a GR10 plaque and waterpoint on the corner of the Hôtel de Ville, to the right. The tourist office, with toilets, and Maison de la Randonée with GR10 displays are along the front to the right. Banyuls is on the railway connecting Spain to Perpignan.

FACILITIES FOR STAGE 55

Banyuls-sur-Mer

Banyuls is a busy tourist resort. The tourist office website lists one campsite and eight hotels, but they're often fully booked in the summer, so make advanced reservations.

Tourist office: tel 04 68 88 31 58, www.banyuls-sur-mer.com

Camping Municipale la Pinède: tel 04 68 88 32 13, www.campinglapinede-banyuls.com

Hôtel Canal: tel 06 01 83 95 33

Hôtel les Pêcheurs: tel 04 68 88 02 10

Hôtel le Catalan: tel 04 68 88 02 80, www.hlecatalan.com

APPENDIX A
Route summary table

Stage	Start stage	End stage	Distance km	Ascent m	Descent m	Time hr:min	Total dist km	Total time hr	Total ascent m	Page
1	Hendaye-Plage	Olhette	21	1200	1100	06:05	21	6	1200	39
2	Olhette	Ainhoa	21	700	700	05:25	42	12	1900	46
3	Ainhoa	Bidarray	21	800	800	05:45	63	18	2700	51
4	Bidarray	Saint-Étienne-de-Baïgorry	16	1300	1300	06:15	79	24	4000	56
5	Saint-Étienne-de-Baïgorry	Saint-Jean-Pied-de-Port	20	900	900	05:05	99	29	4900	61
6	Saint-Jean-Pied-de-Port	Gîte d'étape Kaskoleta	17	900	400	04:55	116	34	5800	66
7	Gîte d'étape Kaskoleta	Gîte d'étape Chalets d'Iraty	20	1400	700	06:20	136	40	7200	70
8	Gîte d'étape Chalets d'Iraty	Logibar	17	500	1400	05:00	153	45	7700	74
9	Logibar	Sainte-Engrâce (Senta)	25	1200	900	07:20	178	52	8900	79
10	Sainte-Engrâce (Senta)	Refuge Jeandel	12	1200	200	04:40	190	57	10100	83
11	Refuge Jeandel	Lescun	15	400	1200	05:25	205	63	10500	87
12	Lescun	Etsaut	16	800	1100	05:25	221	68	11300	92
13	Etsaut	Gabas	25	1600	1200	07:50	246	76	12900	98

Stage	Start stage	End stage	Distance km	Ascent m	Descent m	Time hr:min	Total dist km	Total time hr	Total ascent m	Page
14	Gabas	Gourette	23	1500	1200	08:55	269	85	14400	104
15	Gourette	Arrens-Marsous	15	900	1300	05:10	284	90	15300	110
16	Arrens-Marsous	Refuge d'Ilhéou	20	1600	500	06:50	304	97	16900	115
17	Refuge d'Ilhéou	Cauterets	8	0	1100	02:15	312	99	16900	121
17A	Refuge d'Ilhéou	Pont d'Espagne (via Col de la Haugade)	10	400	900	04:10				125
18	Cauterets	Refuge des Oulètes de Gaube	15	1400	100	06:05	327	105	18300	127
18A	Cauterets	Luz-Saint-Sauveur (via Col de Riou)	22	1300	1500	06:55				131
19	Refuge des Oulètes de Gaube	Chalet-refuge la Grange de Holle	21	800	1400	07:05	348	112	19100	135
20	Chalet-refuge la Grange de Holle	Luz-Saint-Sauveur	26	700	1500	07:45	374	120	19800	140
21	Luz-Saint-Sauveur	Barèges	12	800	300	04:30	386	124	20600	146
22	Barèges	Refuge-Hôtel de l'Oule	23	1300	700	07:45	409	132	21900	150
23	Refuge-Hôtel de l'Oule	Vielle-Aure	17	400	1400	04:40	426	137	22300	155
24	Vielle-Aure	Germ	13	1200	700	04:35	439	141	23500	160
25	Germ	Lac d'Oô	16	1200	1000	06:00	455	147	24700	164
26	Lac d'Oô	Bagnères-de-Luchon	19	1000	1900	07:00	474	154	25700	168
27	Bagnères-de-Luchon	Artigue	8	600	0	02:35	482	157	26300	174

Stage	Start stage	End stage	Distance km	Ascent m	Descent m	Time hr:min	Total dist km	Total time hr	Total ascent m	Page
28	Artigue	Fos	21	1100	1800	06:50	503	164	27400	177
29	Fos	Refuge de l'Etang d'Araing	18	1700	300	06:25	521	170	29100	182
30	Refuge de l'Étang d'Araing	Eylie-d'en-Haut	8	300	1300	03:05	529	173	29400	186
31	Eylie-d'en-Haut	Maison du Valier	17	1600	1700	08:10	546	181	31000	189
31A	Eylie-d'en-Haut	Bonac	15	700	1000	05:40				193
32	Maison du Valier	Esbintz	18	1200	1300	07:10	564	189	32200	195
32A	Bonac	Esbintz	25	1200	1100	07:00				200
32B	Col de la Core	Estours Valley	12	300	1000	03:35				203
33	Esbintz	Refuge d'Aula	19	1200	500	06:05	583	195	33400	205
33A	Esbintz	Saint-Lizier-d'Ustou	20	800	900	06:30				209
34	Refuge d'Aula	Rouze	16	700	1300	04:30	599	199	34100	213
35	Rouze	Saint-Lizier-d'Ustou	7	600	800	03:00	606	202	34700	216
36	Saint-Lizier-d'Ustou	Aulus-les-Bains	23	1400	1400	09:05	629	211	36100	219
37	Aulus-les-Bains	Refuge des Étangs de Bassiès	11	1200	300	05:05	640	216	37300	224
38	Refuge des Étangs de Bassiès	Marc	11	100	800	03:20	651	220	37400	227
39	Marc	Goulier	26	1500	1400	09:10	677	229	38900	231
40	Goulier	Siguer	13	500	800	03:05	690	232	39400	238
41	Siguer	Plateau de Beille	23	2400	1300	09:40	713	242	41800	242

Stage	Start stage	End stage	Distance km	Ascent m	Descent m	Time hr:min	Total dist km	Total time hr	Total ascent m	Page
42	Plateau de Beille	Refuge du Rulhe	14	1000	600	04:40	727	246	42800	247
43	Refuge du Rulhe	Mérens-les-Vals	12	500	1600	04:20	739	251	43300	250
44	Mérens-les-Vals	Refuge des Bésines	10	1300	300	04:30	749	255	44600	256
45	Refuge des Bésines	Refuge des Bouillouses	18	600	700	05:35	767	261	45200	259
46	Refuge des Bouillouses	Planès	19	200	700	04:10	786	265	45400	263
47	Planès	Refuge du Ras de la Carança	15	1200	900	05:45	801	270	46600	267
48	Refuge du Ras de la Carança	Mantet	11	600	900	04:00	812	274	47200	271
49	Mantet	Refuge de Mariailles	15	1100	900	05:15	827	279	48300	275
50	Refuge de Mariailles	Refuge des Cortalets	18	1000	600	05:55	845	285	49300	279
51	Refuge des Cortalets	Gîte-refuge de Batère	17	300	900	04:15	862	289	49600	283
52	Gîte-refuge de Batère	Gîte d'étape l'Ecogîte de la Palette	19	700	1500	06:10	881	295	50300	286
53	Gîte d'étape l'Ecogîte de la Palette	Las Illas	22	1000	1100	07:00	903	302	51300	290
54	Las Illas	Col de l'Ouillat	27	1000	600	06:15	930	308	52300	294
55	Col de l'Ouillat	Banyuls-sur-Mer	24	700	1600	06:50	954	315	53000	299

APPENDIX B
Facilities table

Restaurant/café suggests meals for non-residents. In addition, most gîtes d'étape and chambres d'hôtes will have meals for residents.

Stage	Time between facilities on main route (hr:min)	Location	Hotel or chambres d'hôtes	Gîte d'étape or manned refuge	Bothy	Campground	Food shop	Restaurant or café	Tourist office
1	0	Hendaye-Plage	✓	✓		✓	✓	✓	✓
	1:45	Biriatou	✓					✓	
	2:20	Col d'Ibardin	✓				✓	✓	✓
	1:10	Venta Inzola						✓	
	0:50	Olhette	✓	✓				✓	
2	1:30	Col des Trois Fontaines			✓				
		La Rhune (off-route)							
	1:15	Sare	✓	✓				✓	✓
	2:40	Ainhoa	✓	✓		✓	✓	✓	✓
3	2:50	Col des Veaux		✓					
	2:55	Bidarray	✓	✓		✓	✓	✓	
4	0:30	Saint-Étienne-de-Baigorry	✓	✓		✓	✓	✓	✓
5	4:35	Lasse	✓						
	0:30	Saint-Jean-Pied-de-Port	✓	✓		✓	✓	✓	✓
6	3:45	Estérençuby	✓	✓				✓	
	1:10	Kaskoleta		✓					

Stage	Time between facilities on main route (hr:min)	Location	Hotel or chambres d'hôtes	Gîte d'étape or manned refuge	Bothy	Campground	Food shop	Restaurant or café	Tourist office
7	4:30	Chalet Pedro	✓		✓			✓	
		Gîte d'étape Chalets d'Iraty		✓			✓	✓	✓
8	5:00	Logibar	✓	✓			✓	✓	
		Larrau (off route)	✓	✓		✓	✓	✓	
9	6:35	Gorges de Kakouéta							
	0:45	Sainte-Engrâce	✓	✓				✓	
10	4:10	Col de la Pierre-St-Martin	✓		✓				
	0:30	Arette-la Pierre-St-Martin		✓				✓	✓
11	3:00	Cabane du Cap de la Baitch			✓				
	1:10	Refuge de l'Abérouat		✓					
	1:15	Lescun	✓	✓			✓	✓	
12	0:20	Camping du Lauzart		✓		✓			
	1:25	Plateau de Lhers		✓		✓			
	3:30	Borce	✓	✓			✓	✓	
	0:10	Etsaut	✓	✓	✓		✓	✓	
13	3:30	Cabane de la Baight de St-Cours		✓					
	2:50	Refuge d'Ayous		✓					
	1:30	Gabas	✓				✓	✓	
14	8:55	Gourette	✓	✓				✓	✓

Stage	Time between facilities on main route (hr:min)	Location	Hotel or chambres d'hôtes	Gîte d'étape or manned refuge	Bothy	Campground	Food shop	Restaurant or café	Tourist office
15		Col de Soulor (off-route)						✓	
	5:10	Arrens-Marsous	✓	✓		✓	✓	✓	✓
16	1:40	Estaing		✓		✓	✓	✓	
	1:20	Lac d'Estaing	✓					✓	
	3:50	Lac d'Ilhéou		✓					
17	2:15	Cauterets	✓	✓		✓	✓	✓	✓
18	1:10	La Raillère						✓	
	1:45	Pont d'Espagne/Refuge du Clot	✓	✓				✓	✓
	0:55	Lac de Gaube						✓	
	2:15	Refuge des Oulètes de Gaube		✓				✓	
18A		Reine Hortense						✓	
		Grust	✓	✓				✓	
		Sazos	✓			✓		✓	
		Luz-Saint-Sauveur	✓	✓		✓	✓	✓	✓
19	2:30	Refuge Baysselance		✓				✓	
	1:55	Gave d'Ossoue			✓				
	2:40	Chalet-refuge La Grange de Holle		✓				✓	
		Gavarnie (off route)	✓	✓		✓	✓	✓	✓
20	1:40	Gîte d'étape Le Saugué		✓				✓	

Stage	Time between facilities on main route (hr:min)	Location	Hotel or chambres d'hôtes	Gîte d'étape or manned refuge	Bothy	Campground	Food shop	Restaurant or café	Tourist office
	4:15	Sia				✓			
21	1:50	Luz-Saint-Sauveur	✓	✓		✓	✓	✓	✓
		Viella (off-route)		✓				✓	
	4:30	Barèges	✓	✓		✓	✓	✓	✓
22	1:00	Tournaboup ski area						✓	
	2:25	Refuge d'Aygues Cluses		✓				✓	
		Chalet-Hôtel du Lac d'Orédon	✓	✓					✓
	4:10	Refuge-Hôtel de l'Oule	✓	✓				✓	
23		Refuge du Bastan (off-route)		✓					
	4:40	Vielle-Aure and Bourisp	✓			✓	✓	✓	✓
		Saint-Lary-Soulan (off-route)	✓	✓		✓	✓	✓	✓
24	1:15	Azet	✓	✓				✓	
	2:20	Loudenvielle	✓			✓	✓	✓	✓
	1:00	Germ	✓	✓				✓	
25	1:35	Cabane d'Ourtiga	✓		✓				
	3:10	Granges d'Astau		✓				✓	
	1:15	Refuge du Lac d'Oô		✓				✓	
26		Refuge d'Espingo (off-route)		✓				✓	

Stage	Time between facilities on main route (hr:min)	Location	Hotel or chambres d'hôtes	Gîte d'étape or manned refuge	Bothy	Campground	Food shop	Restaurant or café	Tourist office
	5:20	Superbagnères	✓					✓	
	1:40	Bagnères-de-Luchon	✓			✓	✓	✓	✓
27	2:35	Artigue	✓	✓				✓	
28	1:10	Cabane de Saunères			✓				
	3:05	Cabane des Courraux			✓				
	0:25	Cabane d'Artigue			✓				
29	2:10	Fos	✓	✓				✓	
	0:45	Melles	✓	✓				✓	
	3:55	Cabane d'Uls			✓				
	1:45	Étang d'Araing	✓		✓			✓	
30	3:05	Eylie-d'en-Haut		✓					
31	3:00	Cap de l'Empaillou			✓				
	1:00	Cabane de Grauillès			✓				
	1:50	Cabane de Besset			✓				
	0:50	Cabane Clot du Lac			✓				
	0:35	Cabane du Trapech			✓				
	0:10	Cabane de l'Artigue			✓				
	0:45	Maison du Valier	✓	✓	✓			✓	
31A		Col des Cassaings							
		Bonac	✓	✓		✓		✓	
		Sentein (off-route)							✓
32	2:05	Cabane d'Aouen			✓				
	2:40	Cabane d'Eliet			✓				

Stage	Time between facilities on main route (hr:min)	Location	Hotel or chambres d'hôtes	Gîte d'étape or manned refuge	Bothy	Campground	Food shop	Restaurant or café	Tourist office
	1:35	Cabane de Tariole			✓				
	0:40	Gîte d'étape Esbintz		✓					
32A		Les Bordes-sur-Lez						✓	
		Ayet (off route)	✓					✓	
32B		Cabane de la Subera			✓				
33		Seix (off route)	✓			✓	✓	✓	✓
	1:10	Aunac		✓					
	0:35	Moulin Lauga						✓	
		Pont de la Taule (off route)	✓					✓	
	4:20	Refuge d'Aula			✓				
33A		Trein-d'Ustou	✓						
34	3:25	Ferme les Bouriés				✓		✓	
	1:05	Rouze		✓		✓			
35	3:00	Saint-Lizier-d'Ustou	✓	✓		✓	✓	✓	
36		Bidous (off-route)		✓				✓	
		Guzet-Neige (off-route)					✓		✓
		Prat-Matau (off-route)							
	3:15	Col d'Escots		✓			✓	✓	
37	5:50	Aulus-les-Bains	✓			✓	✓	✓	✓
	5:05	Refuge des Étangs de Bassiès		✓				✓	✓
38		Auzat (off-route)					✓	✓	✓

Stage	Time between facilities on main route (hr:min)	Location	Hotel or chambres d'hôtes	Gîte d'étape or manned refuge	Bothy	Campground	Food shop	Restaurant or café	Tourist office
		Vicdessos (off-route)				✓	✓	✓	
	3:20	Marc		✓					
39	0:15	Mounicou		✓				✓	
	1:40	Refuge de Prunadière			✓				
	3:50	Étang d'Izourt			✓				
		Refuge d'Étang Fourcat (off-route)		✓				✓	
	3:25	Goulier		✓				✓	
40	3:05	Siguer		✓					
41	4:10	Cabane de Courtal Marti			✓				
	0:20	Cabane de Balledreyt			✓				
	2:50	Cabanes de Clarans			✓				
	1:55	Cabane d'Artaran			✓				
	0:25	Plateau de Beille		✓				✓	
42	4:40	Refuge du Rulhe		✓				✓	
43	4:20	Mérens-les-Vals				✓			
44	0:15	Le Soula		✓				✓	
	4:15	Refuge des Bésines		✓				✓	
45	5:35	Lac des Bouillouses	✓	✓				✓	✓
46	0:30	Estany de la Pradella		✓	✓				
	2:00	Bolquère	✓				✓	✓	
	0:30	Col de la Perche	✓					✓	

Stage	Time between facilities on main route (hr:min)	Location	Hotel or chambres d'hôtes	Gîte d'étape or manned refuge	Bothy	Campground	Food shop	Restaurant or café	Tourist office
47	0:50	Planès	✓	✓				✓	
	2:25	Refuge de l'Orri			✓				
	3:20	Refuge du Ras de la Caranca		✓				✓	
48	2:55	Refuge de l'Alemany			✓				
49	1:05	Mantet	✓	✓				✓	
	1:50	Py	✓	✓			✓	✓	
	3:25	Refuge de Mariailles		✓	✓				
50		Abri Aragó (off-route)			✓				
	4:00	Refuge de Bonne-Aigue			✓				
51	1:55	Refuge des Cortalets		✓				✓	
	2:00	Abri du Pinatell			✓				
	0:35	Refuge de l'Estanyol			✓				
	1:40	Gîte-refuge de Batère		✓					
52	2:55	Arles-sur-Tech	✓				✓	✓	✓
	3:15	Gîte d'étape l'Ecogîte de la Palette		✓				✓	
53	7:00	Las Illas	✓	✓				✓	
54	3:30	Le Perthus	✓	✓			✓	✓	✓
	2:45	Col de l'Ouillat		✓				✓	
55	1:30	Refuge de la Tagnarède			✓	✓			
	5:20	Banyuls-sur-Mer	✓				✓	✓	✓

APPENDIX C

Sources of information

BIBLIOGRAPHY

Other Cicerone walking guides to the Pyrenees

The GR11 Trail by Brian Johnson

Pyrenean Haute Route by Tom Martens

Walks and climbs in the Pyrenees by Kev Reynolds

The Pyrenees by Kev Reynolds

Interesting journals/blogs on the GR10

www.pyreneanway.com/french-pyrenees-gr-10-walk-guide
A website giving a lot of practical information, including GPS tracks.

www.pyrenees-refuges.com
A superb resource lisitng pretty much every refuge, cabin and camping area in the Pyrenees. French only.

www.gr10.fr
An indespensible French language guide to the GR10.

Information on mountain refuges

The French Alpine Club site gives up-to-date information on mountain refuges
www.ffcam.fr

Weather

Official French weather forecasts can be found at www.meteofrance.com but the forescasting can be a bit hit and miss. A more reliable resource is www.meteoblue.com

Severe weather warnings for Europe
www.meteoalarm.eu

Historical and current snow depths at a number of French Pyrenees ski resorts which may help planning if you are contemplating an early season hike
www.onthesnow.co.uk

Travel information

Brittany Ferries
www.brittany-ferries.co.uk

P&O car ferries
www.poferries.com

National Express coaches
www.nationalexpress.com

FlixBus coaches
www.flixbus.co.uk

Eurostar
www.eurostar.com

French rail network
sncf-connect.com

RyanAir
www.ryanair.com

British Airways
www.britishairways.com

Air France
www.airfrance.com

Easyjet
www.easyjet.com

Telephone codes

Emergency telephone number: 112

International telephone codes
UK 44 (0044 UK from France)
France 33 (0033 from UK)
Spain 34 (0034 from UK)

LISTING OF CICERONE GUIDES

For full information on all our
guides, books and eBooks,
visit our website:
www.cicerone.co.uk

CICERONE

Trust Cicerone to guide your next adventure,
wherever it may be around the world...

Discover guides for hiking, mountain walking, backpacking,
trekking, trail running, cycling and mountain biking, ski touring,
climbing and scrambling in Britain, Europe and worldwide.

Connect with Cicerone online and find inspiration.

- buy books and ebooks
- articles, advice and trip reports
- podcasts and live events
- GPX files and updates
- regular newsletter

cicerone.co.uk